IN-HOUSE TEAM

Editor: Mike Toller

Features editor: Alexi Duggins

Senior editorial assistant: Joly Braime

Editorial and production assistant: Alix Fox

Editorial assistance: Anton Tweedale, Claire Gardiner, Kelsey Strand-Polyak, Katy Georgiou

Designer: Sarah Winter

Design assistance: Caitlin Kenney, Sara Gramner

Picture research: Alex Amend

Production consultant: Iain Leslie

Web editor: Cameron J Macphail

National ad sales: Sue Ostler, Zee Ahmad

Local ad sales: Catherine Burke

Distribution: Nativeps

Financial controller: Sharon Evans

Managing director: Ian Merricks

Publisher: Itchy Group

© 2007 Itchy Group

ISBN: 978-1-905705-13-9

...per,
...Grossmeier, Bas
...na Yalazi Dawani, Mario Alberto

Illustrations: Tom Denbigh, Si Clark, Joly Braime

Cover illustration: Si Clark (www.si-clark.co.uk)

Itchy Group
White Horse Yard
78 Liverpool Road
London, N1 0QD
Tel: 020 7288 9810
Fax: 020 7288 9815
E-mail: editor@itchymedia.co.uk
Web: www.itchycity.co.uk

Welcome to Itchy 2007

You lucky thing, you. Whether you've bought, borrowed, begged or pinched it off your best mate's bookshelf, you've managed to get your mucky paddles on an Itchy guide. And what a guide it is. If you're a regular reader, you're probably already impressing your friends with your dazzling knowledge of where to head for a rip-roaring time. If, on the other hand, you're a trembling Itchy virgin, then get ready to live life as you've never led it before. We've spent the last year scouring Bath for the very best places to booze, cruise, schmooze, snooze and lose ourselves to the forces of pleasure. As ever, we've made the necessary, erm, sacrifices – in the name of our research – dancing nights away, shopping 'til we flop and of course, eating and drinking more than we ever thought possible. But we're still alive, and now we're ready to do the whole lot again. Come with us if you're up for it – the first round's on us...

KEY TO SYMBOLS

- 🕐 Opening times
- 🍴 Itchy's favourite dish
- 💲 Cost of a bottle of house wine
- 💷 Admission price

Welcome to Bath

It's a big year for Bath, is this. They've finally got the Thermae Bath Spa open after 28 years, and now the meeeja are buzzing about what a great place this is to visit. But it's not just recently that people have enjoyed coming here.

In the race to become the most famous city with a name related to cleanliness, Bath's clearly far and away the winner (in your face Shower Nozzle, Arkansas).

The Romans toddled over here in the final stages of their great march across Europe, and we imagine that after months of sleeping rough they were smelling a bit ripe by the time they got here. Luckily, there were some handy hot springs and, faster that you could say, 'rather a grand complex of bathing houses with several different pools and a steam room, complete with rather swanky under-floor heating', Bath had become one of the world's first tourist destinations.

Bath's been providing the good and the great with distractions from their mundane lives ever since. The Georgians turned the town into a honey-coloured wonderland, so it's their fault that everywhere you look during the summer months there are colonies of French teenagers, backpacks slung over both shoulders, jaws slack at the thought of their first bath in years (because they're teenagers you understand – far be it from us to suggest that ALL FRENCH PEOPLE SMELL).

But don't let that put you off – they're here for a good reason you know. The city centre might be small enough to dance in the palm of your hand, but that doesn't mean it's not packed with enough pleasures to keep even the most dedicated of hedonists in thrills. And for the more sedate, there are plenty of little winding streets for leisurly ambling and wide parks for lazy lounging, not to mention the odd cosy pub for a relaxing pint or three.

Itchy's trusty team of writers, snoopers and snappers have visited every shop, drunk in every pub, stuffed their gobs in every restaurant and dragged their feet round every single museum and gallery just to bring you this guide. With their help you'll have a great time, and you can make sure that you'll never again find yourself in the Museum of Insect Taxidermy wondering just where it all went wrong.

So what are you waiting for?

Introduction

Two hours in Bath

So you've just stepped off the train and you've got a couple of hours until the next one whisks you off somewhere else. Here's how to occupy yourself.

Starting at the station, walk up Manvers Street 'til you reach Bog Island, so named as it was once the site of Victorian public conveniences. Turn left into York Street and walk until you see Bath Abbey. Before you enter, glance to your left where you will see a large wall – this surrounds the Roman Baths. Jump. You'll catch sight of the murky waters of the Great Bath. Enter the Abbey, and behold the tranquillity. When you leave, walk through the courtyard, taking in the man playing the flute through his nose/man playing the saw/thong wearing man on a unicycle juggling fire, and pass through the columns till you reach Stall Street.

Turn right and head along Milsom Street to George Street, where the Porter (left, across the street) is there for your drinking needs. Next, go out turn right up Gay Street, and you'll happen upon the Circus. Take in John Wood's neo-classical architecture, note the acorns atop each house, and feel the energy of the mythical ley lines. Now spend your final half-hour trying to find the station again.

One day in Bath

We're big on packing as much as possible into a small space at Itchy (just look at the size of our guides). Which is why we've decided to make like Ann Diamond putting on a catsuit and squeeze a revoltingly large amount of content into very tight confines by giving you the best of Bath in just 24 hours. Although our version's probably less wobbly (incidentally, this is one of our favourite sentences to say out loud – give it a go, it'll brighten up your day).

Start your day's activities by having breakfast al fresco at the wonderfully-located Riverside Café, where you can take in the joint delights of Pultney Bridge and the weir. Alternatively, you could try the chilled atmosphere of the Jazz Café in Kingsmead Square.

After you've fortified yourself with brekkie, it's probably best to get the fifteen-hour queue at the Roman Baths out of the way. Use your time here to improve your competitive waiting technique, and to discern the best way of deporting the omnipresent French exchange students (our suggestion's loading a trebuchet with high-grade brie to lure them in, then pulling the cord to fire those surrender monkeys back over the channel). When you have finished at the Baths, have a quick nose around the Abbey or take tea in the Pump Rooms if you'd rather, then head up to George Street for a bite to eat at the Adventure Café.

The afternoon should be a time for quiet reflection (mainly about the people in that queue you'd like to have strangled). If the weather's permitting, then make like the Kinks and spend it lazing on the lawn in front of the Royal Crescent. Alternatively, ape the *Monty Python* boys and take a flying visit to the Circus. Suitably rested, get your elbows out for a poke round the shops – particularly Jolly's, which is easy to get lost in. If you're not the shopping type (hello there unenlightened fellas), try one of Bath's many walking tours, which are full of little anecdotes to impress your friends with, in a 'did you know that Beau Nash…?' style. Finish your day with a gentle picnic next to the river in Parade Gardens.

Come the evening, you should head to the famous Moles club, where bands from Oasis to Radiohead to the 5,6,7,8's have all graced the stage at some point. The line-up's almost certainly going to contain a couple of decent bands, so you can cram two evenings' worth of great live music into one fun-packed night.

And that, ladies and gentlemen, is it. NB – Some of our advice regarding the French shouldn't be taken literally if you value your freedom.

Eat

Eat

CAFÉS

Adventure Café and Bar

5 Princes Buildings, George Street
(01225) 462 038

Bath's elevated pavements kept Georgian ladies' dresses above the dirty streets, and displayed them to hot cavalry officers. Adventure Café plays similar roles. Lifting café culture away from greasy spoons to the higher realms, the menu is like a piñata of goodies waiting to be burst open; try open sandwiches the size of huge verdant fields, iced mochas or maple syrup pancakes. It seems to attract people that look good enough to eat, too. Sit out, and tuck in.

☻ *Mon–Wed, 10am–5pm; Thu–Sat, 10am–12am; Sun, 10am–11pm*
🍴 *Gourmet sandwiches, around £4.95*

Bar Chocolat

3 Argyle Street
(01225) 446 060

There's probably a fancy name for a pathological fear of chocolate; whatever it's called, if you suffer it, you should certainly steer clear of this café. The clue's in its name; this place dishes out the chocolatiest chocolate delicacies ever conceived. Think dark chocolate and raspberry milkshakes, double dark choc hot chocolates and the richest Savoy truffles you can imagine. Hell for your waistline or those who have a Freudian phobia about the colour brown, but to others it could well be an early vision of what heaven might look like.

☻ *Mon–Sat, 9am–6pm; Sun, 11am–5pm*
🍴 *Dark chocolate and raspberry milkshake, £3.50*

Boston Tea Party

19 Kingsmead Square
(01225) 313 901

This is one of those little miracles: a chain that has remained refreshingly individual. In Bristol and Exeter its older incarnations have become local favourites. Ergo, the formula works. Brilliant all year round, tables outside add to the appeal of this already cool café. They do a nice line in originally-named sandwiches and wraps along with daily specials, and if you look in their in their drinks cooler you'll find freshly-squeezed juices and old-style ginger ale, plus all the usual suspects. This is a great place to grab a quickie, or spend some quality time with a café you'll grow to love.

☻ *Mon–Wed, 8am–6pm; Thu–Sat, 8am–9pm*
🍴 *Double chocolate brownie, £1.95*

The Fine Cheese Co Café

29 & 31 Walcot Street

(01225) 483 407

Apparently, Bath has an 'artisan' quarter. Other than a shop selling bongs to teenage boys, a couple of pubs where people with dreadlocks drink, and an overpriced vintage boutique, this café is probably the most 'artisan' thing in the area. Posh sarnies with ingredients sourced from the the deli next door, classy little sweet nibbles and totally great coffee make this the perfect place to take parents when they come to town. Plus the tables on the street let you observe the rich, (not very) culturally diverse slice of life that is Walcott Street.

Ⓒ *Mon–Fri, 9.30am–5.30pm;*

Sat, 9am–5.30pm

Ⓘ *Crayfish and rocket sandwich, £4.50*

The Real Italian Ice Cream Company

17 York Street

(01225) 330 121

Little Itchy loved Enid Blyton. Characters named Fanny and Dick had us chortling hot milk out of our noses every bedtime, in Faraway Tree stories featuring a machine that made any ice cream imaginable. It seems this Italian family inherited it, and now whip up iced delights by the scoop or tub, flavoured with tiramisu, pistachio, hazelnut, and the only green apple gelato available outside Harrods, plus shakes, trifles, really real coffee, chocolates, and deliciously authentic accents that might make you want to lick the staff too. Magical.

Ⓒ *Mon–Sun, 10am–late*

Ⓘ *Green apple ice cream cone, £1.60*

Metropolitan Café

15 New Bond Street

(01225) 482 680

Almost exclusively the hangout of middle-aged ladies halfway through doing their shopping on a Saturday, this is an underrated café, right in the very centre of town. They make what could arguably be called the best chocolate milkshake in Bath, possibly the South West. With its homemade, GM-free, organic array of veggie sandwiches and cakes (no pork gateaux here), and slightly odd interior decoration – inspirational/funny quotes by well-known academic types adorn the walls – we love Metro. You couldn't get more 'Bath' if you put on a purple frock and took your friend Ethel out for tea.

Ⓒ *Mon–Sat, 9.30am–5.30pm*

Ⓘ *Goats' cheese ciabatta, £5.95*

Eat

Café Retro

18 York Street

(01225) 339 347

Bare wooden tables? Check. Staff whose nonchalance borders on rudeness? Check. Trendy, slightly dishevelled boho clientele that like to smoke chic little French fags that produce smoke that looks 'simply amazing' in that black and white film their friend Hugo is making? Check. But wait, before you flee headlong from the posey musings, nasal accents and lingering threat of poetry in the air, take a moment, grab a table when you get a chance, and enjoy some of the best café-type food Bath has to offer.

◐ *Mon–Sat, 9am–6pm;*

Sun, 10am–6pm

⑪ *Big fry-up, £6.50*

Riverside Café

17 Argyle Street

(below Pultney Bridge)

(01225) 480 532

Set on what has regrettably become a bit of a tourist route down to the riverboats, this tiny restaurant is nonetheless one of Bath's best-kept secrets. With the best view of the weir in town, not only does this gem serve up a great array of dishes from round the globe, but it's also fully licensed. Tall people – in fact, quite short people as well – beware: the door is a similar height to most dolls' houses. It'll get you every time, especially of you've got stuck into a bottle of their house plonk.

◐ *Sun–Wed, 9am–5pm; Thu–Sat, 9am–9pm*

⑪ *Mexican enchilada, £7.50*

❷ *£12.95*

RESTAURANTS

Ask

Broad Street

(01225) 789 997

What? Another trendy Italian restaurant in Bath? And you're sure it's not another Pizza Express rip-off? Does it have pleasant, but slightly minimal décor? Little red flowers on the tables? Nice, efficient, but a little bit snooty staff? Unmanageably huge bowls of really quite delicious pasta for a good price? Fabulous thin-crust pizza? Sounds a bit familiar, but hey, there's a reason why we go back to places like this.

🕒 *Mon–Sun, 12pm–12am*

🍴 *Paese di pollo e pesto (pizza with chicken, goats' cheese and pesto), £7.75*

🍷 *£11.95*

Bathtub Bistro

2 Grove Street

(01225) 460 593

The day Itchy got our A-level results, we crashed our dad's car and went to this restaurant for the first time. No prizes for guessing which of the two experiences was the more pleasurable. Even if something much better than walloping headlong into a Volvo had happened to us, we think eating at the Tub would have been hard to top. While the place caters handsomely for the flesh-haters among you, it's not afraid to offer some hearty meaty treats for those with a bloody tooth.

🕒 *Mon–Sat, 5.30pm–10.30pm*

🍴 *Field mushrooms with olives and mozzarella, £8.45*

🍷 *£12.50*

The Bath Tap

19–20 St James Parade

(01225) 404 344

Their chef cooked for Princess Di; Itchy's mum said she'd belt us if we made any puns about Meals on Wheels. The grub's royally brilliant though, especially the phone-ahead pre-order service. Their fresh coffee and mighty breakfasts are fit for a king too – and all his horses and men, and could even put us back together again after a heavy night on the tiles. But maybe not if our mum had gotten to us.

🕒 *Bar, Mon–Wed, 10pm–11pm; Thu–Sat, 12pm–2am; Sun, 12pm–10.30pm; Food, Mon–Fri, 7am–5pm; Sat, 10am–5pm; Sun, 12pm–5pm*

🍴 *Breakfast of kings, £4.95*

🍷 *Half bottle champers, £7.50*

Bistro Papillon

2 Margaret's Buildings

(01225) 310 064

Get a table outside in the summer, order some red wine and shut your eyes. You can easily imagine you are in some lovely Provençal town, chatting away to your old friend Pierre about the charming game of boules you had that morning. Open them again and you are back in Bath. But then again, what with the cobbled square before you and delicious, French-inspired food on your plate, who really cares where you are? Exactly. So anyway Pierre, did you see how close I got with that last ball? Not bad for a rosbif, eh?

🕒 *Tue–Sat, 12pm–2.30pm & 6pm–10.30pm*

🍴 *Roast duck magret, £14.95*

🍷 *£9.90*

Eat

Blackstone's Restaurant

2–3 Queen Street
(01225) 444 403

Blackstone's is new, self-consciously stylish and into real food. Ok, the bright pink and green tables might be a bit much if you're in there the morning after the night before, but the muffins and coffee are great and Blackstone's full fry-up is the moon on a big stick. All-day food goes along the lines of a daily soup and bread, as well as more serious eating options such as rib-eye steak or smoked haddock fishcakes. And their veggie dishes sound nice, if you can face greens after those tables.

🕒 *Tue-Sat, 10am–10pm; Sun, 10am–4pm*
🍴 *Brown cow organic beef burger with gruyere, aioli and chips, £10*
💷 *£12*

Curry Mahal

31 Belvedere, Lansdown Road
(01225) 789 666

We much preferred the old name of this place. There was something infinitely satisfying about going to a restaurant called Curry 2000. Memories of the millennium bug and S Club 7 just flooded back every time you saw the sign. And you could sing an altered version of a Pulp track when you wanted to visit, no matter that it made you sound like a Cock(er). They might have changed their name to something more 'traditional' now, but everything else is the same. Which is a good thing as the food here has always been amazing.

🕒 *Mon–Sun, 12pm–2pm & 6pm–11.30pm*
🍴 *Chicken shahjahani, £6.75*
💷 *£9.95*

Circus Restaurant

34 Brock Street
(01225) 318 918

What a location. Slap bang between two of Bath's most picture-postcard-famous bits of architecture, The Royal Crescent and The Circus. Its positioning might mean you think this is going to be an overpriced tourist trap, full of Japanese sightseers taking pictures of their lunch, but you'd be very wrong. This restaurant has a series of excellent set menus which mean you can eat several courses of delectable modern bistro food and still have enough money to get your date a horse-drawn carriage ride back home, or something similarly romantic and mushy. Not peas.

🍴 *3 course set dinner, £17.95*
💷 *£11.45*

Demuth's Vegetarian

2 North Parade Passage
(01225) 446 059

When you've been making vegetarian food for nigh on 20 years you'd hope you would have picked up some skills along the way. The people at Demuth's certainly have. They started cooking meat-free dishes when Maggie was still bashing miners and haven't ever lost sight of their goal: to be the best cow-sparing restaurant in the South West. With an ever-changing menu that brings the most exciting vegetarian, organic and vegan fare to your table they've probably succeeded. Just don't let them know – complacency is no friend to progress.

🕒 *Sun–Fri, 10am–10pm; Sat, 9am–10pm*
🍴 *Beetroot and goats' cheese soufflé, £14.95*
💷 *Organic house wine, £12.75*

The Desh

10 Chelsea Road

(01225) 314 413

Walking into this little local Indian can be an odd and daunting experience. The way they've done it up makes you think that you might have somehow gone back in time and are entering an Italian circa 1982. Push through this moment of doubt though, and you'll discover what we think is the best Indian food you'll find in Bath. The menu is tasty and traditional and, because you can bring your own booze, you should be able to dine like a Keralan king on a tenner before you rev up the De Lorean to go back home.

- *Mon–Sat, 6pm–11pm*
- *Chicken mon pasand, £5.95*
- *BYO*

Eastern Eye

8a Quiet Street

(01225) 422 323

When you're searching for the perfect location for your amazing new Indian restaurant, you might not see a vast, disused ballroom and think, 'Yes, that'll be more spot on than *101 Dalmatians* with acne.' But, fortunately for all concerned, the good people from The Eastern Eye thought like that and have since then managed to create an eatery that not only routinely serves up stunning food for your delectation, but also looks not unlike a Bollywood Panic! At the Disco video. Brilliant? Eye, it is.

- *Mon–Sun, 12pm–2.30pm & 6pm–11.30pm*
- *Chicken mon pasand, £8.90*
- *£12.95*

Eat

FishWorks

6 Green Street

(01225) 448 707

If there is one golden rule for choosing a restaurant when you're not sure where to go, it must be to never eat in a place which displays pictures of its food on the walls. FishWorks on the other hand, display the food you're about to eat in their street-level fishmonger, so you can be sure that what your getting is going to be worthy of your mouth. Head past the glistening catch to the cosy upstairs restaurant and get ready to devour some of the delicacies you saw only minutes ago. Prices depend on what's been caught.

Ⓒ *Tue–Sat, 12pm–2.30pm & 6pm–10.30pm; Sun, 11am–5pm*

Ⓞ *£11.95*

Green Park Brasserie

Green Park Station

(01225) 338 565

She's got a ticket to ride, she's got a tikka with ri-i-ice... The grown-up Braz, housed in the old station booking hall, is just the ticket if you're choo-choosy about posh nosh. Prices aren't off the rails though, especially with the free parking and an early bird menu. It's popular for weddings, which gives you an idea of the elegant, traditional décor and upmarket dishes. Catch live jazz Wednesday to Saturday evenings, or wake up stylishly with a morning coffee and cake in the internet café. Chuffing brilliant.

Ⓒ *Tue–Sat, 10am–11pm; lunch, 12pm–2.45pm; fixed price dinner, 6pm–7pm*

Ⓜ *Stuffed squid, £13.95*

Ⓞ *£10.95*

Hole in The Wall

16 George Street

(01225) 425 242

This is one of Bath's most elegant eateries. The food is brilliant, with a menu that strikes a rare balance between gourmet and the recently popularised 'proper food' craze. We'd better warn you though – this isn't a place for those on a tight budget. Their name must relate to the cash point you won't be able to visit for a fortnight afterwards and might equally be replaced with 'Hole in Your Stomach Through Which The Kidney You Sold To Eat Here Was Removed'. Real nice though.

Ⓒ *Mon–Sat, 12pm–3pm & 6pm–10pm (Sat, 10.30pm); Sun, 6.30pm–9.30pm*

Ⓜ *Whole roast partridge, £16.95*

Ⓞ *£10.95*

Il Tocco D'Italia

Spring Gardens Road

(01225) 311 184

A new and modern take on Italian cooking, right in the heart of traditional old Bath? Something must be afoot. Everything about this restaurant, from its unique, shed-like architecture to the stylish downstairs bar, should have ensured it was shunned by locals. Yet it has thrived. Maybe Bathonians aren't as conservative as everyone thought, or maybe they just love the great Italian nosh. Whatever it is, it's so popular you'll have to book, which is a damn good recommendation really.

Tue–Sat, 12pm–2.30pm & 6pm–10.30pm (open Sundays during the summer)

Ham hock with butter beans, £12.95

£13.90

Moon and Sixpence

6a Broad Street

(01225) 460 962

Blink and you'll miss it. This kind of hidden entrance bodes well for whatever is inside. Think of Alice's rabbit hole, exclusive cocktail bars or the cupboard under the stairs with lost treasure in it. Now you can add this Bath restaurant to the admittedly short list. The archway takes you into a courtyard full of calm; a relief from the busy shopping street you've just escaped. Well-prepared and executed food ensures that this place remains popular with first-daters as well as women weighed down with shopping bags after a hard morning's graft.

Mon–Sun, 12pm–10.30pm

Duck breast with rosti, £16.50

£12.95

Java

39 Gay Street

(01225) 427 919

If this place was a horse it would be a pure-breed with impeccable parentage. It would probably win loads of races and then be put out to stud and command huge prices for his valuable services. Eager young mares would tremble to see his... Sorry, we got a bit carried away there. What we're trying to say is that this place is the real deal; owned and run by people who genuinely come from Java and are really passionate about the food they cook. The décor might be a bit naff but when it tastes this good, who cares?

Mon–Sat, 12pm–2.30pm & 6pm–11pm; Sun, 6pm–10.30pm

Thai green curry, £6.50

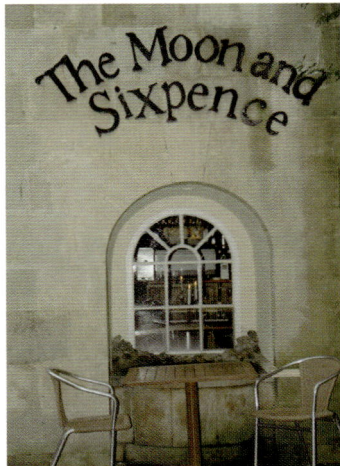

£11

Eat

No. 5 Bistro

5 Argyle Street
(01225) 444 499

Another bistro stakes its place in the heart of the city. Yaaaaawn. But wait – this one looks a bit different. Where are all the overcooked steaks? What's all this tasteful decoration and romantic lighting? Did we read that right: on Wednesdays they specialise in fresh fish? This is something more than a bog standard brasserie, and what's more it's a BYO some of the time, so you can drink your bottle of £1.99 wine while eating in palatial surroundings. No 5 is alive, and no mistake.

🕒 *Mon–Sat, 12pm–2.30pm & 6pm–10.30pm*
🍴 *Sauté of lamb's sweetbreads and mushrooms in pastry, £7.45*
🍷 *Mon–Tue, BYO*

The Olive Tree

Russel Street
(01225) 447 928

This place really is the bee's knees for foodies. The ever-changing menu, always delivers the best seasonal and local produce. There's a price to pay for this gastronomic indulgence however, quite literally: The Olive Tree doesn't come cheap. But, our mum always said you get what you pay for, and mums are always right. This is the place to treat a special someone (like your mum perhaps). Or, better yet, have someone (mum?) treat you – everything tastes better when you're not paying.

🕒 *Mon–Sun, 6pm–10.30pm*
🍴 *Panfried scallops with pumpkin and vanilla puree and chorizo oil, £10.50*
🍷 *£14.50*

Peking Chinese

-2 New Street, Kingsmead Square
(1225) 461 750

s a general rule, Chinese restaurants utside world cities and China itself are abitually something of a disappointment. While other national cuisines travel well, ere seems to be something about Chinese ood that means it becomes greasy, alty and expensive whenever it makes provincial appearance. Fortunately, ath's Peking Chinese is by no means e worst Chinese restaurant to grace our hores. If you have a hankering for various ny courses that somehow leave you avenously hungry 20 minutes after paying e bill you could do a lot worse than here.

◉ *Mon–Sun, 12pm–2pm & 6pm–11.15pm*
❶ *Half a crispy aromatic duck, £19.95*

Rajpoot

4 Argyle Street
(01225) 466 833

We like Indian restaurants that give you a bowl of Bombay mix as soon as you sit down. All those unidentifiable crunchy things always put us in a great mood. They also ensure that even if the food that follows is inedible you're so stuffed with those tiny dry pea wotsits that it doesn't matter. Rajpoot, however, offers the best of both worlds, with Indian food so good that it's almost worth resisting the temptation to gorge on random bits of spicy stick and save room for an extra side dish.

◉ *Mon–Thu & Sun, 12pm–2.30pm & 6pm–11pm; Fri–Sat, 12pm–2.30pm & 6pm–11.30pm*
❶ *Lamb rezala, £8.95*
❷ *£12.95*

Fried and tested

There are some times when you should never try and get a decent early morning feed in Bath. Like New Year's Day. We tried, and ended up up eating something dreadful on Abbey Churchyard. Don't ever go there. Luckily, any other day of the year there are plenty of good places to kill your hangover. For a proper café experience, **The Waverley** café (Kingsmead Square) opens early and serves massive, heart attack-inducing portions. The cafés in **BHS** and **Morrisons** are very cheap, as you pay by the item, though the food's not exactly tops and there's a risk you'll be sharing a table with your gran. The **Adventure Café** and **Same, Same But Different** offer a slightly classier caff experience, essential when that 'special' person you met last night isn't as grim as you'd feared.

Eat

Ring O'Bells

10 Widcombe Parade

(01225) 448 870

If the term 'gastropub' usually makes you reach for the nearest firebomb, give this place a chance before you plan your next incendiary attack. Managing to strike the right balance between traditional boozer and foodie hangout, the Ring o'Bells treads the line between cool and try-hard that so often foxes other similar places. Plus, Massive Attack once played a secret gig upstairs, which keeps us coming back in the hope it might happen again.

☻ *Mon–Sun, 6pm–11pm*

🍴 *Portobello mushroom stuffed with spinach, mascarpone cheese and toasted pine nuts, £9.80*

✪ *£11.50*

The Walrus and Carpenter

28 Barton Street

(01225) 314 864

A topsy-turvy shabby-chic cult den since 1974, making family recipes from locally-sourced and organic ingredients, with mountains of veggie fare and walloping sides of loveable bonkersness. Breaks the mould, and proves with aplomb that mould is never what you want associated with your food anyway. The name comes from a nonsensical Lewis Carroll poem, penned after scoring opiates. Itchy doesn't recommend chasing the dragon; he'll never lead you to this glorious place.

☻ *Mon–Sat, 12pm–2.30pm & 6pm–11pm; Sun, 12pm–11pm*

🍴 *Burger with mustard & apple sauce, £8.85*

✪ *£14.50*

Same, Same But Different

7a Princes Building

(01225) 466 856

Not just a pretty face (though the management do seem to have a slight penchant for hiring only attractive females as members of staff), this café also has a serious weight of culinary intellect behind its broad smile. By day, tapas and sandwiches will do nicely if you like things a bit Iberian; by night, it becomes the sort of bar you wish you'd found on holiday, instead of that horrible place full of English hockey teams and sick and Nadia Sawalha making a daytime BBC documentary about Brits abroad.

☻ *Mon–Wed, 8am–6pm; Thu–Fri, 8am–12am; Sat, 9am–12am; Sun, 10am–5pm*

🍴 *Calamares à la romana, £4.50*

Woods

Alfred Street
(1225) 314 812

As we all know, Bath is full of rugby clubs, but this is probably Bath's only real rugby restaurant. Being Bath, we're not talking greasy post-play pie here either. This is something all together classier. On Saturdays you'll find the place packed with the sporting lawyers and accountants who've been at the match enjoying rather delicious French bistro food. They will also all be secretly hoping that the owner will have one of his famous outbursts and throw someone out. Why don't you come down and, err, try it.

Mon–Sat, 12pm–2.30pm & 6pm–10pm
Pan fried duck breast, £16.95
£13.95

Yak Yeti Yak

12a Argyle Street
(01225) 442 299

Back in the day, a nuked steak at the Bernie Inn was considered a good meal out. Nowadays, your discerning diner wants a bit more from his eating experience. Step up Yak Yeti Yak, Bath's finest (albeit first) Nepalese eatery. Serving up great food that's somewhere in between Indian and Thai, in a subterranean room that makes you believe you're under the Himalayas, this is a really unusual place that will make you look oh-so-sophisticated when you bring your hot new date. Join the Yak-cult now.

Mon–Sat, 12pm–2.30pm & 6pm–10.30pm;
Sun, 12pm–2.30pm & 6pm–10pm
Yak Yeti Yak beef, £7.50
£11.50

Food for nought

Getting hold of some free food in Bath is tricky. None of the churches run free lunch programs and getting food from Julian Road homeless shelter is really just heartless. Unless you're homeless, of course. The only hope is the myriad of food-based festivals and stuffing your face with samples. Between the end of November and December, **The Abbey Churchyard** is transformed into a picturesque Christmas market and, if you look doe-eyed enough, you're sure to pick up some donated nosh. Throughout the spring and summer, **Queen's Square** has a French-style market. Hit it at closing and offer to take the ripest cheese and nearly stale bread off their hands. You'll get a tasty meal, even if it'll stop you kissing anyone for about a week.

Test of moral fibre

ALRIGHT, SO WE'RE ALL SUPPOSED TO BE EATING ETHICALLY NOWADAYS. BUT WHAT WE WANT TO KNOW IS WHETHER ANY OF THE MONKEYS THAT BANG ON ABOUT THIS STUFF HAVE EVER TRIED IT OUT WHEN PICKING UP SOME POST-PUB STOMACH FILLERS. IT'S A BLOODY NIGHTMARE. OBSERVE:

Illustration by Si Clark, www.si-clark.co.

1 **Food miles** – According to some environmental fascist or other, it's not ecologically friendly to eat stuff that's been flown across the world when you could chomp on courgettes grown much closer to home. Not according to our friendly burger van, however.

Itchy: 'Excuse me, but how many food miles has that quarter pounder done?'

Burger man: 'What?'

Itchy: 'How many miles has it travelled to end up here?'

Burger man: 'Ten miles, mate. Straight from Lidl to this spot.'

Itchy: 'But what about where it came from originally? What about the sourcing?'

Burger man: 'Saucing? I've got ketchup and mustard, you cheeky sod. And it's free, not like him down the road and his "10p-a-sachet" bollocks, now you gonna buy this burger or what?'

'Reckon you could catch enough fish for all the UK's chippies using a fishing rod?'

2 **Sustainability** – It's not meant to be the done thing to eat fish caught in a way that stops our scaly friends reproducing fast enough to prevent their numbers dropping. Sadly, no-one's told our local chippy.

Itchy: 'Is your cod line-caught?'

Chippy owner: 'Yeah, it's caught mate. How else do you reckon it comes from the sea?'

Itchy: 'No, I'm asking if it was caught using a fishing rod.'

Chippy owner: 'You reckon you could catch enough fish for all the UK's chippies using a fishing rod?'

Itchy: 'Erm, no...'

Chippy owner: 'Right, well there's your answer then.'

Itchy: '...but, you know that you should only really eat fish from sustainable sources don't you?'

Chippy owner: 'Oh yeah? According to who? The media? Reckon all that coke they're on's organic? Produced locally, is it?'

Itchy: 'Well, it's not always possible to consume entirely ethically…'

Chippy owner: 'My point exactly.' One cod and chips then is it?'

Drink

Drink

BARS

Adventure Café and Bar

5 Princes Buildings, George Street
(01225) 462 038

One of Bath's best chill-out café bars. The policy is all things bright and beautiful: staff, drinks, food. With a continental feel, the lights may be dim in the evenings but the clientele glow. Musically, it's a hot spot for those who prefer a retro classic re-hashed to a dub-step beat over whatever cheddar DJ Sammy has vomited into a bucket, spread onto vinyl and attempted to market. Putting the 'vent' back into 'adventure', this place is a breath of swanky fresh air.

☻ *Mon–Wed, 10am–5pm; Thu–Sat, 10am–12am; Sun, 10am–11pm*

❷ *£11.50*

All Bar One

11–12 High Street
(01225) 324 021

Over-21 bars. The final frontier. No students, which means no drinking games, no raucous shouting, no 'sexy' dancing, no vomit on the floor. During the day, All Bar One serves a pan-European menu of tapas, 'big plates' and burgers, and during the night it becomes a hub of sophistication where over-21s quietly debate the nature of existentialism and sip moderately-priced wine. Or so we're told.

☻ *Mon–Sat, 11am–11.30pm; Sun, 11am–11pm; Food, Mon–Sat, 11am–10pm: Sun, 11am–9pm*

❶ *Tapas, £4 for one plate, £11 for three, £20 for six*

❷ *£10.90*

Beau Bar

34 Monmouth Street
(01225) 460 962

On Saturday nights you risk being deafened by the baying laughter of the play-watching types who flock to this bar before and after shows at the nearby Theatre Royal. Not that we've anything against thesps, but to be honest it can all get a bit overbearing. However, come to Beau Bar anytime when there isn't a performance and you'll discover a bar that is both warm and individual. Which makes a nice change in a city where a 'Vodka Bar' franchise is considered the height of drinking sophistication.

☻ *Mon–Sat, 12pm–11pm; Sun, 12pm–10.30pm*

❷ *£11.50*

Belvedere Wine Vaults

25 Belvedere
(01225) 330 264

It's sad and all that most of Bath's traditional pubs are being systematically turned into wine bars. But when the conversion is as good as this one it's only those frumpy blokes who like real ales and trains who bother to complain. What was a grotty pub has been transformed into a friendly bar, with great food and shed loads of nice wine. Well-stocked with 45 different types of vodka, this place is at the top of a hill so after a visit here you'll finally understand the term 'rolling drunk'.

🕐 *Mon–Sat, 12pm–11pm;*
Sun, 12pm–10.30pm
🍴 *Cured meat plate, £8.50*
💷 *£11*

Browns

Orange Grove
(01225) 461 199

Browns always seem to find wonderful locations for their restaurant-bars; the one over in Bristol is in the old student refectory, while Bath's outlet used to be a magistrates' court. Grand architecture aside, you know exactly where you are with Browns: subtle lighting and décor, lots of pot plants and greenery and the slight feeling you could be anywhere at all in the Western world. At least you know the portions of food will be massive and the cocktails will be adequate, which, if you think about it, is a fitting metaphor for Western society.

🕐 *Mon–Sun, 11am–11pm*
🍴 *New York Caesar salad, £9.50*
💷 *£11.50*

Drink

Central Bar

10 Upper Borough Walls
(01225) 333 939

A smart, vibrant bar with an upstairs lounge more relaxed than Frankie when he finally got to Hollywood. The dazzling cocktail list, with monthly specials, is as long as one of your grandad's war stories, and staff relish the challenge of whizzing together any kooky concoction you can dream up. Inspired by the black pool table, Itchy invented a Slow Comfortable Screw against the Baize (or 'Milfshake' for short). Excellent Illy coffee and upmarket grub too. Central-sational. Unlike our dire puns.

🕐 *Mon–Sun, 12pm–11pm; Food, Mon–Fri, 12pm–3.30pm; Sat–Sun, 12pm–4pm*
🍴 *Goats' cheese salad, £5.95*
💰 *£10.95*

The Common Room

2 Saville Road
(01225) 425 550

A few years ago this place would have died a quick death and no-one would have even noticed that it had come and gone. But now all those happy people who used to go to Po Na Na every weekend are in their late twenties and want something classier than overpriced beer and sixth-form girls being loudly sick in the toilets. So the Common Room is a sort of hybrid late bar/club where a man with a trendy haircut plays records from the 60s and people might dance if they're in the mood and they finished the week up on the stock exchange.

🕐 *Mon–Wed, 6pm–1am; Thu–Sat, 6pm–2am*
💰 *£12*

Delfter Krug

Sawclose

(01225) 443 352

The huge terrace here is more essential in summer than factor 50 sunblock is for gingers, and their excellent music policy ensures that you'll burn, baby, burn on the dancefloor until the early hours too. With a delectable selection of wines and beers, a cosy retro interior and gourmet pies that paste paltrier pastries, DK fuses good taste and good fun better than Kinder Eggs ever could, even those ones with little models of cute frogs. This place doesn't need to be kissed – it's already a prince.

🕐 *Mon–Thu, 12pm–2am;*
Fri–Sat, 12pm–3am
🍴 *Minty lamb pie, £4.90*
💷 *£10.90*

Drink

Grappa Bar

3 Belvedere

(01225) 448 890

Old Bathonians are up in arms about this place. It used to be a proper spit and sawdust cider pub, full of the old classics of years gone by, but now it's a trendy and intimate wine bar, packed with those annoyingly self-righteous 20-somethings who like to talk loudly about how successful they are. So why don't we hate it? Well it's well-stocked with alcohol, and their pizzas are really rather good. Just don't mention our views to anyone who looks like they used to enjoy bright orange cider that could make you go blind.

☻ *Mon–Sat, 5pm–11pm; Sun, 6pm–10.30pm*

🍴 *Buffalo mozzarella salad, £4*

🍸 *£13.95*

Lambrettas

8–10 North Parade

(01225) 464 650

Should really be in Brighton we suppose, but at least Bath begins with a B, so it's sort of the same in a not-at-all kind of way. How many terrible puns can we shoehorn into a 50 word review of this 'mod' themed bar?...MODified from your typical hotel drinking spot, allowing people to drink with a MODicum of comfort, this place offers all the MOD cons you'd expect from a MODern bar. You could say it was the perfect MODel for a boozer, except the prices are far from MODest. Still, if you don't drink with MODeration you'll get hamMOD.

☻ *Mon–Sun, 11am–11pm*

🍴 *Loaded BLT, £4.95*

🍸 *£12.95*

Ha Ha

The Tramshed, Beehive Yard

(01225) 421 200

'Laughter is a unique expression of the typical tension between the 'vital' and the spiritual (known by intuition), on the one hand, and the mechanical and the material (known through the intellect), on the other', said a Mr. David Heyd. Ha Ha takes this tension between the vital and mechanical, feeds it chunky chips and burgers then gives it half-priced cocktails after six. Intuition and intellect are much obliged.

☻ *Sun–Wed, 10am–11pm; Thu–Sat, 10am–12am; Food, Mon–Sat, 11am–10pm; Sun, 11am–9.30pm*

🍴 *Chargrilled vegetables and goats' cheese wrap, £5.95*

🍸 *£9.95*

Lounge

43 St James Parade

(01225) 424 321

Somewhat out of the way, this venue's atmosphere certainly makes it worth a teensy detour from the bright lights of Bath's pub and bar scene. Slick in the extreme, with all the usual trappings of an über-trendy refurb: leather couches, mirrors, chic tables and chairs, and beautiful boys and girls serving cracking cocktails. However pretentious this all sounds, it actually remains a great place for a relaxed and slightly more sophisticated drink. Don't be scared off if you have a ratty beard, one eye and a parrot; everyone is really friendly and ready to cater for anyone.

☻ *Mon–Sun, 11am–11pm (sometimes later)*

🍸 *£11.95*

The Porter

15 George Street

(01225) 424 104

A miracle of modern science. Forget deluded boffins trying to grow earlobes on the back of terrapins, The Porter is an incredibly comfortable pub/bar hybrid with more added superpowers than Teen Wolf has bad hair days. They have an all-vegetarian menu wider than Mr McGregor's allotment, comedy on Sundays, and free live music on weeknights. Not that you'll ever have another weak night again.

🕐 *Mon–Thu, 11.30am–1am; Fri–Sat, 11.30am–2am; Sun, 12pm–11.30pm; Food served 'til 9pm*

🍴 *Spinach lasagne with chips, veg or rice, £5.75*

💷 *£9*

porter

15 George Street - Bath
www.theporter.co.uk

Bath's only totally Vegetarian pub also offers fantastic FREE live music during the week, DJs at the weekends and the famous Comedy Cavern (with Student concessions) on Sunday night

Drink

St James' Wine Vaults

St James Square

(01225) 310 335

Although we can't verify the rumours that this is the new hangout of Johnny Depp and his trendy chums, we can divulge that it's the chosen lair of a diverse yet harmonious range of locals – from the rather intimidating man covered in tattoos to, well, lots of student types. Upstairs you'll find a traditional pub frequented by said locals; downstairs, a cellar bar that often plays host to private parties and world music nights, and a friendly ghost who is said to pop up now and then to greet lonely barmaids… The sly dog.

🕐 *Mon–Thu, 2pm–12am; Fri–Sat, 2pm–1am; Sun, 2pm–10.30pm*

💷 *£11*

PUBS

The Ale House

1 York Street

(01225) 400 088

It's rare to find a pub that understands the meaning of 'value' and doesn't confuse it with 'cheap'. The Ale House bobs along in a lovely, relaxed manner during the day, but really starts buzzing come the evenings. Their roast is less than a fiver and closer to heaven than several saints (especially St Hubert, the mollusc fondler). Open all week, with pool, darts, and a welcome warmer than a pair of Totes toasties.

🕐 *Mon–Fri, 11am–12am; Sun, 12pm–10.30pm; Food, 12pm–2.30pm*

🍴 *Cod and chips, £3.45*

💷 *£6.50*

The Bath Tap

19–20 St James Parade
(01225) 404 344

Soaper, smashing, great. Perch yourself on one of the lather... sorry... leather seats in any one of the three bars (that scrubbed up jolly nicely after last year's refurb), enjoy home-cooked food washed down with some bubbly or ale, and soak up the entertainment, which ranges from karaoke every other Friday to drag acts and burlesque. The owners here really put in the effort and take pride in running an all-welcome, good-vibes pub, and it shows. Good times on tap.

🕐 *Mon–Wed, 10am–11pm; Thu–Sat, 12pm–2am; Sun, 12pm–10.30pm; Food, Mon–Fri, 7am–5pm; Sat, 10am–5pm; Sun, 12pm–5pm*

The Bell Inn

103 Walcot Street
(01225) 460 426

Dreadlocks and a slightly warped sense of style are compulsory here. Located smack-bang in the middle of Bath's 'Artisan Quarter', anything goes – especially on Walcot Nation Day in July, when the Bell suddenly comes over all patriotic by becoming the central drinking den during the festivities. Expect ageing hippies, lots of people who do their weekly shop at Harvest just down the road, lots of real ales (along with the beardy real ale buffs that go with them), and an outgoing, easy atmosphere.

🕐 *Mon–Sun, 11.30am–11pm; Sun, 12pm–10.30pm*

💷 £8.50

Drink

The Boater

9 Argyle Street
(01225) 464 211

Greek myth tells of Charon, ferryman of the dead, punting the damned across to hell. Bath's Boater has the more enviable job of setting souls sailing on their merry way to heaven, via two-pint bottles of fantastically-named cider 'Natch'. Itchy's slightly deaf mate was surprised it didn't come in a furry cup. Four different levels incorporate newly-refurbed inside bars, a pool area, gargantuan sports screens and the biggest late-license beer garden in the city, with BBQs and footie tournaments in summer. A favourite with the Bath rugby team, and pretty much scrum-ptious all round.

☻ *Mon–Sat, 11am–11pm;*
Sun, 12pm–10.30pm

The George at Bathampton

Mill Lane, Bathampton
(01225) 425 079

This pub might be a couple of miles out of town. But the walk along the towpath is lovely on a sunny day, and the welcome alone is worth the effort. Add to this good beer, pub food, and the option of sitting outside, watching the holidaying families and odd-looking greasy-haired people float by (on their barges; we're not suggesting that people dump bodies in the canal in a sinister, gangster type fashion. This is Bath after all, dahling).

☻ *Mon–Sat, 10am–11pm; Sun, 12pm–*
10.30pm; Food, Mon–Sat, 12pm–10pm;
Sun, 12pm–9.30pm
🍴 *Sunday roast, £7.95*
💰 *£11*

The Grapes

14 Westgate Street
(01225) 310 235

When we were growing up, there was a persistent rumour that this place was a 'transsexual' pub. Quite how the small and conservative population of Bath would support enough transsexuals to warrant a special bar of their own never entered our juvenile heads. But for years we avoided the place, which is a shame because in reality it is an okay pub where you're always guaranteed to get a seat. To this day, Itchy has never spotted a transsexual in Bath, apart from on *Hollyoaks*, and that doesn't count.

☻ *Mon–Sat, 12pm–11pm;*
Sun, 12pm–10.30pm
💰 *£10.95*

The Hobgoblin

47 St James Parade
(01225) 460 785

Crazy rockers and melancholy goth kids listen up. It's very unlikely you'll find any pink shirts here. Ditto for footballer wannabes in horribly tight clothing and naff haircuts. Instead you'll find the hardmen of rock; never smiling and always drinking. The liquids on offer are as potent as the hormonal angst. Hardcore local brews and drinks with special powers dominate. The only difficulty is negotiating the crowd of pierced-up (boom boom) teenagers outside trying to pluck up the courage to have a go at getting served.

☻ *Mon–Sat, 11am–11pm;*
Sun, 12pm–10.30pm
❷ *£8.50*

The Huntsman

1 Terrace Walk
(01225) 482 900

It's important to have a gimmick. If there's something quirky about your bar, no matter how watery your beer or odious your staff, people will come flocking to your establishment. The Huntsman's gimmick is that you can get in here when anywhere else that serves alcohol after 11pm is full. Naturally, this means the people drinking here are a rag-bag bunch of young-looking girls and bladdered boys on stag dos. Still, if you really can't face bed without a little nightcap, you know their door will always be open.

☻ *Mon–Wed, 12pm–11pm; Thu–Sat,*
12pm–2am; Sun, 12pm–10pm
❷ *£12.95*

Games for a laugh

If you are worried that you don't really like your so-called "friends" all that much, choose a pub with plenty of other distractions so you won't have to bother with actually talking to each other. **The Raven** has a wide selection of board games for you to play. Alternatively, **St. James' Wine Vaults** runs a rather fun quiz on a Thursday night which is only £1 to enter and there are prizes for a top 3 finish, so you could easily find yourself with booty. Maybe you're in the city centre on a Sunday night and are just gasping for a good testing. Well you're in luck, as **The Crystal Palace** holds just the ticket. It's fun, loud and gives a justification for having spent all the rest of the day reading the papers and not helping your significant other do whatever he or she was nagging you to do.

Drink

The King William

36 Thomas Street

(01225) 428 096

Bath's gentrification marches on. A few years ago this pub was right in the heart of the town's 'bad neighbourhood', but now it's on just another desirable street within walking distance of the city centre. The King William perfectly reflects the area's change of fortune, turning, Cinderella-like, from rundown dive to poshly painted foodie hangout. After midnight, we've heard it becomes a spit and gravel alkie paradiso, but since it closes at 11pm, no-one's ever actually seen this.

☎ *Mon–Sun, 12pm–11pm;*
Food, Mon–Sun, 6pm-10.30pm
⏷ *Mains from £9*
❷ *£12.45*

The Old Farmhouse

1 Lansdown Road

(01225) 316 162

Growing up, The Farmhouse was the only place that would accept our poorly-faked ID, and though usually deserted, at about 9pm on a Saturday night it would fill to bursting-point. We discovered that The Farmhouse was as famed for its live jazz sessions every weekend as for the fact they'd accept a flimsy piece of paper, hand-written by a dyslexic, as proof of age. Nowadays they're rather more savvy about identification, but the jazz is still wonderful and the locals more than worth joining for a pint and a toe-tap.

☎ *Mon–Sat, 12pm–11pm;*
Sun, 12pm–10.30pm
❷ *£9.95*

The Old Green Tree

12 Green Street
(01225) 329 314

Tiny pubs are usually terrifying places; with not enough room to escape to a quiet corner, you risk being sucked into conversation with that strange man at the bar called Vic or something about when it were all fields as far as the eye could see and he used to ride to school on a unicycle. The Old Green Tree is a little pub, with a large selection of 'real' beer on tap, which all means you might be worried about braving the regulars. But the city centre location seems to have worked some magic on this place, as everyone is friendly, interesting and (relatively) sane.

Mon–Sat, 11am–11pm; Sun, 12pm–10pm
£10

The Pig & Fiddle

2 Saracen Street
(01225) 460 868

Becomes the Fig and Piddle if you've had one or two. Pleasantly located on what the one-way system has turned into a roundabout, this is essentially an extension of the Bath University students' union. A beer garden with a pleasant view of the Hilton Hotel means that it's packed in the summer, and an affinity with sports means that it's packed in the winter, but don't let that put you off: the Pig is raucous, loud, always busy, but great fun.

Mon–Sat, 11am–11.30pm; Sun, 12pm–10.30pm; Food, Mon–Fri, 11am–8pm; Sat, 11am–6pm; Sun, 12am–6pm
Ostrich burger, £5.75
£11.50

Drink

The Ram

20 Claverton Buildings

(01225) 421 938

Wanted: the lost memories from nights spent in The Ram drinking with the very friendly but brutally alcoholic regulars, who like nothing more than taking new faces under their wing, and then getting them so drunk that the ten minute walk back into town can take upwards of 2 and a half hours, and when you do finally get home you seem to have acquired a traffic cone and a pensioner called Stanley along the way. A return visit will mean another jug of 'rough' cider and another round of boisterous drinking games whose rules never become clear.

🕒 *Mon–Sat, 12pm–11pm; Sun, 12pm–10.30pm (open earlier for sporting events)*

The Raven

7 Queen Street

(01225) 425 045

Rising, phoenix-like from the ashes of scary biker-pub, The Hatchet, this place has quickly become boozer of choice for drinkers who are in-the-know. They have a vast selection of local ales which whiskery men in knitted jumpers will tell you are 'very well kept' (whatever that means). For everyone who doesn't spend their Sundays searching for the perfect pint of 'Old Toejam', there are lagers and ciders by the bucket load, as well as delicious pies to soak up some of that booze.

🕒 *Mon–Sat, 11am–11pm;*

Sun, 12pm–10.30pm

🍴 *Chicken and ham pie, £6.95*

💷 *£11.55*

The Saracen's Head

42 Broad Street

(01225) 426 518

SNOBBERY WARNING – CODE RED SNOBBERY – CODE RED... One hundred and fifty years ago, Charles Dickens stayed here while he put the finishing touches to his masterpiece, *The Pickwick Papers*. Unfortunately, whatever attracted big Charlie Boy's attention is long gone, leaving a decidedly average joint, which is filled at weekends with the kind of people who, you suspect, wouldn't know a Dickens novel if you were to take one down off the bookshelf and bludgeon them to death with it.

ⓒ *Mon–Sat, 10.30am–11pm;*
Sun, 12pm–10.30pm

€ *£8.95*

The Star Inn

23 The Vineyards

(01225) 425 072

'Just one of Bath's many old men's pubs', right? Oooooh no. On first glace, it's likely you'd make that same rash judgement as Itchy ourselves made for years. Then our friend's dad made us go in and we fell hopelessly in love. When you realise a good pub isn't one that markets itself with '2-4-1 on Breezers, mini-skirts get in free on a weekend', you'll see that The Star offers everything you'd want in a drinking-hole. It's cosy, friendly and there might even be a little dog to keep you company as you sip your pint. Aaaaaah yes.

ⓒ *Mon–Sat, 11am–11pm;*
Sun, 12pm–10.30pm

€ *£11*

Drink

The Volunteer Rifleman's Arms

3 New Bond Street

(01225) 425 210

The winner of Itchy's award for most evocative pub name ever (sadly no actual prize changes hands though). Just entering makes you think you're on your last days of shore leave, kissing your sweetheart goodbye-ee before heading off to fight for king and country in some far-flung corner of our indomitable empire. No? Maybe it's just us then. For everyone else, this is just a little place in the heart of the city's shopping area. It's a good spot to stop off when hitting the shops gets a bit much.

Mon–Sat, 11am–11pm;
Sun, 12pm–10.30pm
£10.50

The White Hart

Widcombe Parade

(01225) 313 985

Gentrification is a funny thing; The White Hart used to be the pits, a pub that no one would ever thing of trekking out to Widcombe for. Now, thanks to a lick of paint and some tables and chairs salvaged from a jumble sale then savaged down to trendy bare wood levels, it's one of Bath's hottest tickets. The food is excellent but the bar's opening times can be confusingly irregular, despite the fact that they sometimes stretch well into the night.

Mon–Sat, 11.30am–close; Sun,
12pm–10.30pm; Food, Mon–Sat, 12pm–2pm
& 6pm–10pm; Sun, 12pm–2.30pm
Grilled rib-eye steak with green
peppercorn butter, £12

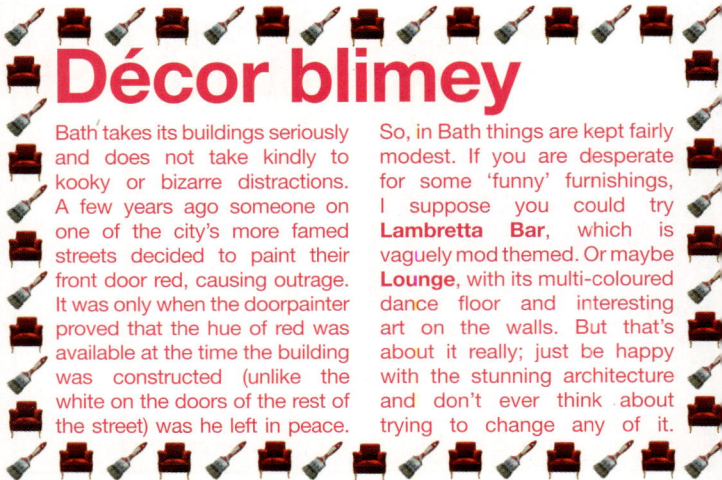

Décor blimey

Bath takes its buildings seriously and does not take kindly to kooky or bizarre distractions. A few years ago someone on one of the city's more famed streets decided to paint their front door red, causing outrage. It was only when the doorpainter proved that the hue of red was available at the time the building was constructed (unlike the white on the doors of the rest of the street) was he left in peace.

So, in Bath things are kept fairly modest. If you are desperate for some 'funny' furnishings, I suppose you could try **Lambretta Bar**, which is vaguely mod themed. Or maybe **Lounge**, with its multi-coloured dance floor and interesting art on the walls. But that's about it really; just be happy with the stunning architecture and don't ever think about trying to change any of it.

Stay regular

Illustration by Joly Braime

AIN'T NOTHIN' QUITE LIKE STEPPING INTO A BAR AND BEING GREETED AS ONE OF THEIR OWN. HERE'S ITCHY'S GUIDE TO BECOMING AS REGULAR AS CLOCKWORK SOMEWHERE NEW

1 Learn the name of the publican's partner/pet/mum – Take a couple of mates and stand at the bar within earshot of the publican and engage in the 'what would your porn name be?' game (combine your pet's name with your mum's maiden name). After a while, get the publican to join in, and make up some new variants designed to extract info about the names of spouses, dad, etc. Next time you walk in, you'll be able to greet them with a friendly, 'Alright Dave, how's Sandra doing?'

2 Have your own pint mug – Take a vessel and ask them to keep it behind the bar for you. Then whenever you walk in, you can sup your beverage in style. You may want to save this for the second visit.

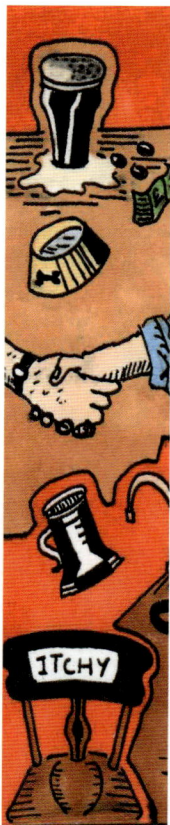

3 Know the pool rules – If they've already got a set of rules in place, learn what they are, loiter near the table and make sure you pounce upon any infraction to loudly proclaim 'That's not how we do things in here'. If there are no house rules, even better – make some up, don't tell anyone what they are, and then soon everyone'll need to ask you before playing.

4 Start a cribbage team – Unless the pub in question's populated by incontinent octogenarians, there's no chance that they'll have one. Get a 'Captain' T-shirt, and swan round asking randoms if they're ready for the big match. They'll have no idea what you're talking about, allowing you to explain your importance to the pub community.

5 Take a dog – Everyone loves a dog. Well, except asthmatics. But who cares about them? Those guys are already having enough of a wheeze.

IF YOU'RE AFTER GUILTY PLEASURES, WHY NOT GO FOR THE OLD CLASSICS? NO, NOT PROSTITUTION AND PICKING YOUR SCABS, BUT CHOCOLATE AND SEX

The first stop on your journey of depravity is **Bar Chocolat** (3 Argyle Street, 01225 446 060), Willy Wonka's factory for grown ups. Stop by for a disgustingly delicious piece of caramel-drizzled, cream-bedecked cake, some hot chocolate or a posh ice cream, and then visit the counter to stock up on goodies to eat at home. WARNING: Itchy cannot be held responsible for you swelling until you can't fit into your clothes or Jerry Springer has to remove a wall of your house to move your fat arse.

If love handles haven't destroyed your libido, then there's only one place to pick up something for a special night in, and that's **Ann Summers** (11a–12 Stall Street, 08700 534 067). No longer a guilty pleasure because of its range of sex toys, but because it's the cheesiest place on the high street to be seen. Beware though, reader, nothing puts you off your new naughty gear like watching a size 24 woman buying crotchless knickers.

Guilty pleasures

Illustration by Si Clark
www.si-clark.co.uk

Dance

Dance

CLUBS

Club X

90b Walcot Street

(01225) 464 241

The name might have changed, and the carpet decorated with horrible pictures of cars and sticky with 1,000 spilt pints and vomit might have been removed, but don't let it fool you; this is still probably as good an image of what Hell looks like on a Saturday night as you'll find anywhere. Still, if you want drinks that cost a quid, a fumble with someone on a hen night and the very real possibility of a fight as you leave, then by all means head down and discover just how right we are when we advise you to avoid this place like the plague.

Ⓒ *Opening times vary*

Delfter Krug

Sawclose

(01225) 443 352

'All the world's a stage, and all the men and women merely players...' Facing the Theatre Royal, Delfter Krug is a fave Itchy playpen, and a stage we don't anticipate growing out of any time soon. Not with such eclectic nights on offer: from 70s pop to hip hop and indie, with special guest DJs and musical taste that's cutting-edge not cut-and-dried, it makes the dismal selection of tunes at other venues look about as varied as the choice of Clarks school shoes for a kid with a club foot. Our foot's through this club's door every time.

Ⓒ *Mon–Thu, 12pm–2am;*
Fri–Sat, 12pm–3am

Ⓔ *Free–£7*

Moles

14 George Street

(01225) 404 445

Not the sort that perches above Chesney Hawkes' upper lip, but very much the underground animal. Party Monday. Party Tuesday. Party Wednesday – you get the notion. Living and breathing music, Moles packs in more catchy live stuff than a bacteria sandwich, as well as knock-out club nights that guarantee an almighty bash. Sausage yourself into a neon spandex unitard for Big Cheese on Tuesday, or if you like your house tidier than Kim and Aggie's, rock up at the weekend. Holy moly, it's what you've been praying for.

Mon–Sun, 9pm–2am; Fri–Sat, 9pm–4am; Sun, 8pm–12.30am

£3–£7

Dance

Po Na Na
7–8 North Parade
(01225) 424 952

For some reason, the vast majority of Bath's clubs are underground sweat holes. Po Na Na is their proud, sweaty overlord: on busy nights (and they all are) you can't move in here without running the risk of tipping your beer all over some hapless shape-thrower. They like to mix it up a bit musically: whilst ordinarily it sticks to the realms of cheesy pop nights – and has the clientele to prove it – Po's occasionally invites the hot-steppers in to one of its rinsin' drum 'n' bass nights. Keep your eyes peeled for posters.

🕒 *Mon & Wed, 9.30pm–2am; Tue & Thu, 10pm–2am; Fri & Sat, 10.30pm–2.30am*

💷 *£12*

Qube
1 South Parade
(01225) 312 800

Bath's newest nightspot and it shows. This club has targeted music lovers with a strictly 'cool' policy on their beats. From urban jams to trembling dance tunes, the DJs really love to try and rip it up. If you like cheap, flat cider that makes you go cross-eyed for weeks (and who doesn't?), head somewhere else. Alternatively, if you want to find out what effect your new designer clobber has on the opposite sex, then this is your Mecca. Drinks prices are surprisingly standard, so you can splash out if you want. And contrary to all of the above, students are welcome, apparently. Bonza.

🕒 *Mon–Sat, 5pm–2am*

💷 *£10*

HEN PARTIES

Distinguishing features: Normally perform their all-female pre-mating ritual in a circular dance around sequined receptacles containing grooming apparel. The leader usually wears a letter L and some kind of sexual apparatus on her head.

Survival: For males under 60, camouflage is the best bet. Itchy recommends a bright pink mini-skirt, padded boob tube and red lippy.

HOMO NARCOTICUS

Distinguishing features: This unusual subspecies is mesmerised by repetitive rhythms and flashing lights, and has a peculiar ability to move all limbs and appendages at once in contrary directions, including eyes and ears.

Survival: These malcos are guaranteed to spill your drink on themselves. Put your bev in a bike bottle or go the whole way and throw a sacrificial pint at them before you start dancing.

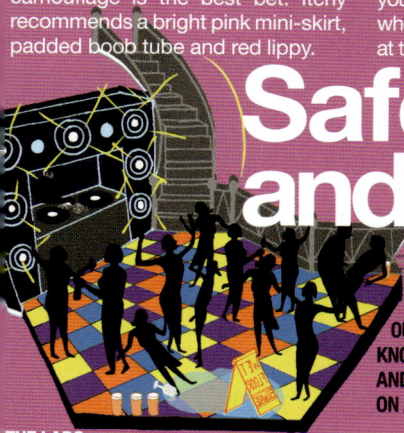

Safe
Illustration by
Thomas Denbigh
and sound

THE DANCE-FLOOR IS A SCARY REALM. IF YOU WANT TO MAKE IT OUT ALIVE, YOU'LL NEED SOME INSIDER KNOWLEDGE, SO GRAB PITH HELMET AND GLO-STICKS AND FOLLOW ITCHY ON A DISCO SAFARI

THE LADS

Distinguishing features: Alpha males indulging in competitive play, such as mixing several beverages in the same glass, and then drinking the whole lot as quickly as possible.

Survival: A propensity to punch the air during power ballads can lead to injury among taller adventurers. Itchy suggests you don a helmet and hit the deck if you hear the line 'Oooh baby do you know what that's worth?'.

UNDERAGE DRINKERS

Distinguishing features: Identified by greasy hair, pale skin and vacant eyes, this genus often regurgitate upon themselves, presenting a hazard to bystanders. Females are impervious to cold and wear very little.

Survival: Enlist their natural predators – larger and more primitive hominids called bouncers, who covet the hair of the underage drinkers, being themselves a furless species.

Itchy

'The tables here are cleaned with the same amount of care that a dog takes wiping its arse.' *Itchy's review of a scummy bar, 2006*

'What?' You're thinking. 'You can't say that...' Oh yes we can. As the most straight talking-est, no-bullshit guide to going out in the UK, we'll never shy away from telling you if somewhere sucks harder than a toothless granny eating a boiled sweet. We also say nice things too.

Gay

Gay

PUBS

The Bath Tap

19–20 St James Parade
(01225) 404 344

The longest established friendly homo from home in the city, with more people out of the closet in its three bars than in a Primark dressing room. Come the weekend it rocks harder than a kid with ADD on a granite rocking horse. Straight folk are more than welcome too; the Tap aren't worried about the angle of your dangle so long as there's a smile on your face and your heart's in the right place. Where you want to put your other bits is entirely up to you.

☻ *Mon–Wed, 10pm–11pm; Thu–Sat, 12pm–2am; Sun, 12pm–10.30pm*

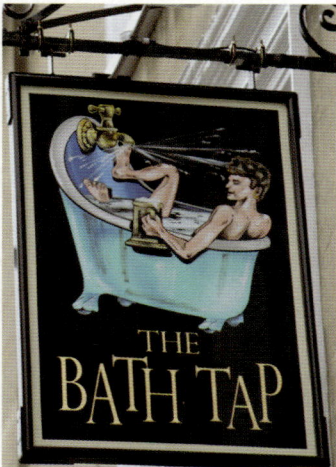

BARS

DYMK

11–12 Westgate Buildings
(01225) 330 470

No, not a rip-off fashion brand, but the undoubted King of Bath's small, but perfectly formed, gay bar scene. There are regular theme nights, with everything from cabaret to bingo keeping people in need of silly distraction happy. For everyone else, the relaxed atmosphere and friendly vibe ensures that repeat visits are a pleasure. FYI: it stands for 'Does Your Mother Know', a bangin' ABBA choon, sung by the boys for once.

☻ *Sun–Thu, 11am–11pm; Fri–Sat, 11am–1am*
💰 *£6.95*

CLUBS

Mandalyns

13 Fountain Buildings, Landsdown Road
(01225) 425 403

An institution. It's an overused phrase, but this bar can probably claim to be one of Bath's finest gay institutions. Offering food, entertainment and a club in the basement this place has a bit of everything, so never say we don't spoil you. Just one thing before you grab your coat and rush out the door; recently there have been reports that the place has become a members-only affair so you'd better get on the phone before heading down.

☻ *Mon–Wed, 3pm–11pm; Thu–Fri, 3pm–12am; Sat, 12pm–12am; Sun, 12pm–10.30pm*

OTHER

The Suite

4 Pierrepont Street

(01225) 465 725

A truly honest, professional, clean venue. Gay, bi, curious or TV, The Suite is less seedy than a good grape, and with a sauna, bar, video screen and privacy rooms, a darn sight fruitier too. Friendly and pressure-free, towels, condoms and lube are in lockers so you don't have to ask. There's even a 'dark room' so you can develop those snaps of your family rambling break in the Peak District. Climb every mounting.

Sun–Thu, 11am–11pm; Fri, 11am–12am; Sat, 11am–3am

Entry, £10; students/concs, £8; 7-day pass, £30

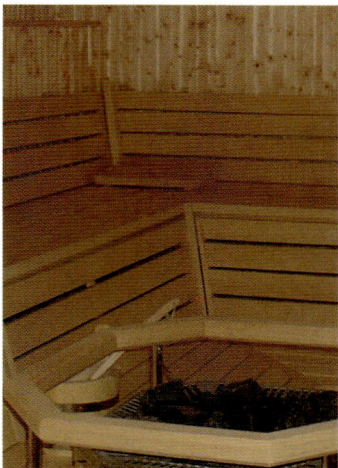

SO YOU'RE A FRIEND OF DOROTHY WHO'S FOUND THEMSELVES IN A NEW TOWN, AND IT MIGHT AS WELL BE THE EMERALD CITY, YOU'RE SO CLUELESSLY GREEN. HOW DO YOU TRACK DOWN THE BEST PINK PLACES? LET ITCHY GUIDE YOUR RUBY SHOES WITH SOME PEARLS OF WISDOM…

Even if their tastes aren't quite yours, they can give you the lowdown on the more subtle gay haunts, and you and Toto will be going loco in no time.

Scally or pally? – Various gay fetishes for chav-style fashions can make

Gay abandoned

There's no place like homo – Just because you're out of the closet doesn't necessarily mean that you love the great outdoors; camping it up isn't for everyone. However, the most kitsch, flamboyant venues are generally well advertised and typically the easiest ones to find; their mass appeal means you usually get a fair old proportion of straights in there too, enjoying their recommended weekly allowance of cheese, but you should have no trouble tracking down a few native chatty scenesters.

it hard to tell a friendly bear pit from a threatening lions' den full of scallies, especially if you've only heard rumours that somewhere is a non-hetters' hot spot. Be cautious in places packed with trackies unless you want your Adid-ass kicked.

Get board – Internet message boards have honest, frequently updated tips; magazines like *Diva* and *Gay Times* have links to local forums on their sites. Click your mouse, not your heels, and get ready to go on a bender.

Illustration by Si Clark
www.si-clark.co.uk

Club 9

ITCHY

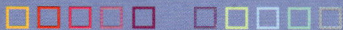

Shop

Shop

DEPARTMENT STORES

Jolly's

13 Milsom Street

(08701) 607 224

Jolly's is Bath's best department store, part of the House of Fraser chain, and the first stop when looking for an outfit for a posh night out. The guys and girls at the MAC counter can offer a shimmering makeover, and the lingerie section will make sure that you avoid hitting the town in something more festering than Uncle Addams. There's a good range of labels and once you've learned the layout you'll be able to go from 'frumpy' to 'hump me' in under 60 seconds. Jolly good.

Mon–Fri, 9.30am–6pm;
Sat, 9am–6pm; Sun, 11am–5pm

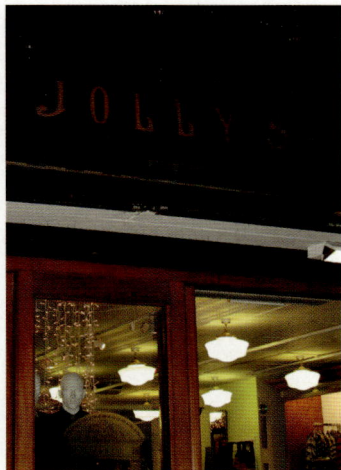

Rossiters

38–41 Broad Street

(01225) 462 227

Specialises in stylish and practical things with which to deck out your spacious townhouse. While you may not be able to afford a designer dining set for your beans on toast just yet, the kitchen section is great for quirky gadgets and pet accessories that make mini poodles look even more ridiculous than their genes already manage. Not somewhere to hang around if you're still young, carefree and so busy going out you eat off paper plates to save time, but if you're the sort who gets themselves in a lather about quality homeware, this place will put the bubbles in your Bath.

Mon–Fri, 9.30am–5.30pm;
Sat, 9am–5.30pm

MARKETS

Guildhall Market

High Street

(01225) 460 808

This is Bath, so don't expect any dodgy geezers trying to sell you 'No Victim, No Crime' posters or knock-off perfumes (sadly, as Itchy have found some corkers in our time - Britney's 'Bi-Curious' and Jean-Paul Gaultier 'Catsuit For Men', for example. We kid you not). Instead you get gems like a deli counter, a secondhand book stall (that buys as well as sells) and a hardware stall with essentials like buckets, light bulbs and mops. Perfect if you don't want your basics gold-plated, and would rather they just do what they say on the tin.

Mon–Sat, 8am–5.30pm

CLOTHING

John Anthony
26–28 High Street
(01225) 424 066

So painfully cool that you already need to have a killer wardrobe just to walk in without getting a laser death ray stare from the staff. Itchy estimates that John Anthony is approximately 73.59% responsible for student debt in the Bath area, as freshers hammer their plastic with the mighty bludgeon of fashion. That's why you'll see so many well dressed girls in September, but they all look a bit scruffy and sprouty by mid-March. Perfect if you like your clothes with someone else's name on them.

Mon–Fri, 9.30am–6pm; Sat, 9am–6pm; Sun, 12pm–5pm

Scallywag
9a York Street
(01225) 445 040

What did we do before jeans? What did one wear when trying to look casual yet hip, irresistible and yet not bothered? Luckily with Scallywag in town we'll never have to face that terrifying prospect. The guys in here can size up your waist and leg measurements in seconds, and hand you the perfect pair, whether you're looking for budget or bling. Then you can go out and waggle your perfectly denim-clad buttocks at as many scowling scallies as you like, and watch as they steam and melt within their velour tracksuits like the Wicked Witch of the West.

Mon–Fri, 9.30am–5.30pm; Sun, 10.30am–4pm

Mee
9a Bartlett Street
(01225) 442 250

Beautiful things for beautiful people. Mee was previously a well-kept secret in Bath, but now word has spread and has even reached celeb shoppers, with references to it popping up in the top glossies. It's no surprise really, given the stock of vintage-style dresses, butterfly garlands, delicate jewellery and gorgeous gifts that you're free to browse through and stroke lovingly without pressure to buy. Come in here for some Mee time; the staff make a genuine effort to pamper you and make you feel welcome, even if you're more Lucy Lichen or Mildred Mould than Kate Moss.

Mon–Sat, 10am–5.30pm; Sun, 11.30am–4.30pm

Shop

Westworld

36 Westgate Street

(01225) 447 006

Westworld stocks the uniform for loan-laden students; Bench, Hooch, Firetrap and all their homies. Itchy remembers when Hooch was not a desirable brand of threads, but a foul lemony alcopop fashionable amongst fag-smoking 12-year-olds hanging about in parks. You could even get a knock-off version from Aldi with a picture of a bulldog on the label: Pooch. No cheap copies here, but a lot of the genuine article packed into the tiny floors. The girls' section downstairs might bring on an attack of intense claustrophobia, but it's still worth risking a panting hyperventilating sweating ferret about in.

🕐 *Mon–Sat, 9am–5:30pm; Sun, 11am–5pm*

SHOES

Office

3 Burton Street

(01225) 466 055

The home of the killer heel, and constantly packed to murderous levels. Stocking funky limited edition trainers, quirky flats and kinky boots, they're bound to toe a nice line in whatever floats your seafaring vessel. Often have deals of the 'buy one, get one half price' variety, so keep an eye on the window for sale posters, and hotfoot it in there to get your high-rise teeter totterers at a low down price. Itchy once misread a sign and ended up in a sex shop thinking it was this place. 'Orifice' didn't have the kind of pumps we were after.

🕐 *Mon–Sat, 9am–6pm; Sun, 11am–5pm*

Silvershoon

11 Upper Borough Walls

(01225) 469 735

Little sister to Shoon over the road, this is the place to go for winter boots or summer Birkenstocks, or if you want names like Ugg, Timberland and Ecco with staff who can offer helpful advice on fittings. Purveyor of the sensible shoe and not the right spot if you wish to turn on your partner with your footwear. Unless of course, the supportive heel and cushioned sole does it for them, in which case Itchy suggests you use it to kick them to the curb. We've seen them perving at OAPs' ankles in beige orthopaedic sandals when you're not looking.

🕐 *Mon–Fri, 9am–5.30pm;*

Sat, 9am–6pm; Sun, 11am–5pm

BOOKS

Mr B's Emporium of Reading Delights

14–15 John Street

(01225) 331 155

The best bookshop in Bath, and possibly the world. Beautiful, friendly, and well stocked, particularly with brilliant fiction and travel writing. If they don't have something they'll order it with almost supernatural speed, and there are regular events like readings and book signings. The staff are happy to recommend books or have a spirited literary conversation, and the chummy shop dog, Vlashka, is a great help when browsing the shelves too. Mr B is grade A.

○ *Mon–Wed & Sat, 9.30am–6.30pm; Thu–Fri, 9.30am–8.30pm*

Waterstone's

4 Milsom Street

(01225) 448 515

There's something about shops with more than one floor that just screams quality. You don't see many Woolworths with elevators and floor guides now, do you? That's right. You don't.

○ *Mon–Sat, 9am–7pm; Sun, 11am–5pm*

WH Smith

6–7 Union Street

(01225) 460 522

Is it a sweetshop? Is it a stationer's? Is it a bookshop? It's whatever you want it to be. So grab a pack of wine gums and some Mills and Boon and stop asking questions.

○ *Mon–Fri, 9am–5.30pm; Sat, 9am–6pm; Sun, 11am–5pm*

Oxfam Bookshop

4–5 Lower Borough Walls

(01225) 469 776

A goldmine of old hardbacks and out-of-print nostalgia, which is ruled by ancient biddies with a sharp glint in their eyes and a frightening knowledge of everything on their shelves. Not the place to pick up the latest bestseller (though you might find several done-with copies of last month's hot read), but great to browse for first editions or pick out an unusual tome from days gone by. As you walk out with your 20-year-old edition of *Fly Fishing* by JR Hartley you can glow with the knowledge that you have done your good deed for the day. And make the old ladies cackle by telling them 'it was this big' – you know they love it.

○ *Mon–Sat, 10am–5pm*

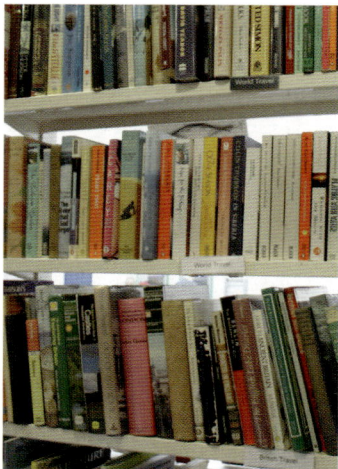

Shop

MUSIC

Fopp
Unit 5–10 Westgate Buildings
(01225) 473 830

Despite the antics of naughty pirates on the interweb, Itchy still likes buying CDs, DVDs and books. Fopp is the only place to purchase your entertainment (excluding Dirty Badger's All-Nude Crack Shack, of course), balancing bargain prices with a great range of stock. There are legendary box sets and copies of cult children's shows that could make a grown nerd weep with joy. Blokes especially can lose themselves, and most of the contents of their wallets, in here for hours. Much better than burrowing away somewhere like Badger's.

🕑 *Mon–Sat, 9am–6pm; Sun, 11am–5pm*

OTHER

Bath Pet Centre
7 Lower Borough Walls
(01225) 461 461

If you never got the hang of that 'making friends' business, and find yourself trying to make conversation with cold callers who just want to sell you double glazing or know what colour your Y-fronts are, then it might be time to invest in a companion. Bath Pet Shop doesn't provide an escort service, but it does sell feathery, furry or fishy friends and everything you need to keep them happy. The knowledgable, chatty staff may even cure your fear of people. For show-offs and allergy sufferers they also stock an impressive range of reptiles.

🕑 *Mon–Sat, 9am–5.30pm*

Bloomsbury
15 New Bond Street
(01225) 461 049

Knick knacks for rich people hungry to spend their zillions on a pigeon-shaped cushion and matching table lamp. Brilliant for presents, provided you have the cheddar in your account; if you can't find a quirky gift for someone in this place you may as well buy them a book token and head home. Stocking everything from individual and funky jewellery to Nigella's range of upmarket kitchenware, it's also a great place to have a browse even if your pockets are empty of all bar fluff. Which you could use to stuff an emu-shaped draught excluder, then sell it for shedloads

🕑 *Mon–Fri, 9.30am–6pm; Sat, 9am–6pm; Sun, 11am–5pm*

Bath Sweet Shop

8 North Parade Passage
(01225) 477 000

Remember the days when happiness was a bag of cinder toffee and a sugar mouse? We don't either; there were far more hyperactivity-inducing E-numbers responsible for Itchy's childhood highs. Relive more wholesome golden days here though for less than £1. There are jars and jars of classics, with old folks looking for a fix of milk bottles and school kids counting out their coins to see if they can afford another gobstopper. Forget recreational drugs and go for sugar; it's a whole lot cheaper, your teeth are the only bits of your face liable to fall off, and even that's preventable with thorough brushing.

⊙ *Mon–Sat, 10am–5.30pm; Sun, 11am–4pm*

Eric Snook's Golden Cot

2 Abbeygate Street
(01225) 464 914

Tired of paying the bills, washing up, going to work every day? Embrace your inner child and head for Eric Snook's, purveyor of toys, games and childhood dreams. It's impossible to be in this store for more than five minutes without squealing at a bat-commanding pitch at the remote control cars, wooden pirate swords and titchy pan pipes. Whether you're babysitting your naughty cousins or rediscovering your own youth you'll love it; after all, you're never too old for an ant farm. If you do find yourself accompanied by one of the little people, let them run wild whilst you examine the *Star Wars* toys or Sylvanian Families.

⊙ *Mon–Sat, 10am–5pm*

Lush

12 Union Street
(01225) 428 271

If you can get over a smell that could stun a horse and that has been likened (in the case of their Red Rooster soap) to the odour of one of those cringey crusty tissues you find slung under the bed many, many mornings after, then this is a fun place to spend a couple of quid to brighten up bath time. Despite all natural ingredients and a strong message of no animal testing, everything in the shop is fluorescent, including the staff's hair, make-up and personalities. Itchy loves the chocolate massage bars, shower gels you set in the freezer, and tubs of freshly-made face goo.

⊙ *Mon–Fri, 9.30am–5.30pm; Sat, 9am–6pm; Sun, 11am–5pm*

Shop

Gash

www.gash.co.uk

When Itchy's mate Dave discovered this über-classy online erotic emporium, stocking lingerie, cosmetics, books, lotions, and lady-pleasing toys including the 'Tongue Joy', he declared, 'That's just like the rhyming kitchen product; Gash – loves the jobs you hate'. This revealed both his dire bedroom prowess and an acute lack of grease-busting knowledge – that's Mr Muscle, not Flash, twazzock. When he's finished with the sink, we've got his girlie some personalised pants to help him patch things up, with a photo of his mug and the words 'Dave, come on down'. Our own deluxe satin pair look stunning, but maybe having them embroidered with 'Itchy' wasn't such a good idea.

Space NK

10 New Bond Street
(01225) 482 804

More make-up than a clown's travelling trunk, and all top names; magic potions from the likes of Nars, Stila, Eve Lom, Bumble & Bumble, Philosphy and Crew to mattify your shiny bits and gloss up dull spots. Whatever your facial issue, something in Space NK will be able to cover it up, soothe it away or burn it off all together. And if you don't think you have facial issues, 20 minutes reading all the labels and jars in this shop will make you realise you're wrong. Pricey, so if you're really ugly, be prepared for some angry letters from HSBC post-NK. If you have skin, they'll make you skint.

🕐 *Mon–Sat, 9.30am–6pm; Sun, 11am–5pm*

IF YOU THINK VEGGIES ARE CRANKY, YOU'LL LOVE THIS. FREEGANS SAY OUR ECONOMIC SYSTEM HURTS THE ENVIRONMENT, TREATS ANIMALS CRUELLY AND WORKERS UNFAIRLY, AND WASTES RESOURCES, SO YOU SHOULDN'T PAY FOR FOOD. IDIOTS. HERE'S HOW WE'D BE FREEGANS…

1. Have a Pret dinner – The bods who run Pret a Manger obviously don't know much about the principles of Freeganism, given how much they throw away each day. Turn up at closing, rummage through their bin bags, and hey presto – free dinner.

2. Kill an animal – Apparently it's legal for you to kill squirrels on your own property. With this in mind, set up a bird table, cover it in superglue and get the pot boiling while you wait for it to become a squirrel lolly. Sure, you might snare the odd bird, but extra protein's always welcome, and the RSPB'll never catch you.

3. Forage – Those in the country could nick apples from trees and scour woodland floors for wild mushrooms. Alternatively, those of us whose parents aren't blood-related to each other could pull half-eaten trays of late-night chips from bins.

4. Mug a milkman – Those bastards don't need all that milk. But you do. Being a freegan isn't conducive to a calcium-rich diet, after all. Wait until your local milky's delivering to a dark area, then knock him out and chug as many bottles as you can before making your getaway.

5. Sniper rifle the zoo – Get up high, and train your gun on the elephant cage. It's not going to be easy to take one of those suckers down with one shot, but if it pays off, you'll be eating like a monarch for weeks. Plus you could sell the tusks on to practitioners of Chinese medicine for extra cash.

Freegan fun

Illustration by Thomas Denbigh

0800700200
FREE
PHONE

G.A.N
SKIP HIRE

Out & about

Out & about

CINEMAS

The Little Theatre

St Michael's Place

(01225) 330 817

Dinner and a movie – it's the best possible first date. Visiting the flicks is great, because if your date has turned out to be as interesting as Graham Taylor you can relax for a couple of hours without having to talk to them. On the other hand, if you like them enough to be thinking of names for your first child, there is always the sneaky yawn-hug combo. And The Little Theatre is exactly the type of cinema you want: independent, intimate and showing the sort of arty films that should make you look cool.

🕐 *Mon–Sun, 10.30am–9.30pm*

🎟 *Adults, £6*

COMEDY

Comedy Cavern

Porter Cellar Bar, George Street

(01225) 424 104

Pub comedy can be one of the most embarrassing things in the world. There is nothing worse than someone standing up, thinking they are hilarious, when in fact they are just telling the room about their last bowel movement or embarrassing sexual encounter. Luckily, The Porter's Comedy Cavern events generally attract a better class of funny people. Jimmy Carr started out here, don't you know? Just make sure you get a seat near the front, but not right at the front, unless you fancy having your urination habits mocked in public.

🕐 *Irregular Sunday evenings; call for details*

The Odeon

James Street West

(08712) 244 007

You know the drill: all the latest blockbuster releases at prices to make you wince; spotty, teenaged ushers who look like they'd rather tear off your head than your ticket stub; weird space age décor; big screens and comfy seats the size of sofas; some annoying kids sitting at the back, eating sweets loudly and talking all the way through the movie. God, we're starting to sound a bit like our grandparents here. Still, you know you'll be able to see some genuine Hollywood magic, and those seats really are very comfortable.

🕐 *Mon–Sun, 11am–9pm*

🎟 *£6.80/£5.60 concessions*

GALLERIES

Beaux Arts

12–13 York Street

(01225) 464 850

This place is really intimidating. We don't know why but for some reason going into this gallery is always a terrifying experience. Maybe it's something to do with the fact that all the paintings are for sale and way beyond our meagre Itchy salaries. It's a shame because the pieces they show here are of the highest quality, including work by some big name artists. And, because the place is blissfully small, you can give each art work the attention it deserves. Just take a few deep breaths and go in. It'll be worth it.

🕒 *Mon–Sat, 10am–5pm*

🎟 *Free*

Victoria Art Gallery

Bridge Street

(01225) 477 772

The Victoria Art Gallery's website is obsessed with the fact that the gallery is home to – and we quote – 'a wonderful array of over 150 china dogs'. Good for them. Good for us that the gallery also houses a chunky selection of decent works by some famed artists, from Turner to Walter Sickert. If you are trying to impress that Swedish exchange student you've just met, you can tell them that Sickert might well have been Jack the Ripper. That little fact, coupled with all those china dogs is sure to impress anybody and make you look awesome.

🕒 *Tue–Sat, 10am–5pm; Sun, 1pm–5pm*

🎟 *Free*

Holburne Museum of Art

Great Pulteney Street

(01225) 466 669

Wandering down Great Pulteney Street on the way to The Holburne, it would be easy to imagine that you've stepped back into a Jane Austen novel, if it weren't for all the massive bright orange buses rushing past every five minutes. Once inside the gallery you'll discover nice old oil paintings of people who are now dead, but who were quite important in making Bath what it is, and have odd names like Beaux Nash. The gallery has another masterpiece too: a lovely tea-shop in beautifully kept gardens, where you can eye up the D'Arcy on the table next to yours.

🕒 *Tue–Sat, 10am–5pm; Sun, 11am–5pm*

🎟 *Adults, £5.50; students, free*

Out & about

MUSEUMS

The Assembly Rooms and Museum of Costume
Bennett Street
(01225) 477 789
Ever wondered how a 16th century socialite dressed? Well this is where you'll find out. Inside there are loads of old clothes from the last 500 years, many of them rather grand. A fascinating inspiration for the budding fashion designer inside all of us. As an added bonus, it's always rewarding to take a sneaky peek at the crazy combinations of clothes the Japanese tourists who fill the museum will inevitably be wearing.
🕑 *Mon–Sun, 11am–5pm*
🎟 *Adults, £6.50*

Mr Bowler's Business
Julian Road
(01225) 318 348
We've never seen anything quite like this place (unless you're counting our living room after a serious house party, that is). Instead of being a bog standard boring museum about the industrial revolution, with lots of stuff in dusty glass cabinets, this is a real factory, with all the junk from an old place of work stacked up in a wonderfully chaotic mess. The aim is to tell the story of a single business and its 100 year history through these artefacts, and they succeed quite wonderfully in doing it. For our part, Itchy was bowler-ed over by it all. Make it your business to go.
🕑 *Mon–Sun, 10am–5pm*

Jane Austen Centre
40 Gay Street
(01225) 443 000
Bath's enduring appeal as a tourist destination over the last few decades owes a lot to the talented Ms Austen and her literary creations, and as such, it's only appropriate that the city has a little museum in honour of the *Pride and Prejudice* author. Inside you'll find displays of how life was back then; outside you are treated to the sight of a bored teenager dressed in period costume trying to entice people in. How anyone could get bored doing that is a mystery to Itchy. Oh, to walk but a few yards in her shoes.
🕑 *Mon–Sat, 10am–5.30pm;*
Sun, 10.30am–5.30pm
🎟 *Adult, £4; concs, £3*

Royal Crescent Museum
1 Royal Crescent
(01225) 428 126
Let's be honest, you are never, not even in a million years, ever going to be rich enough to live on The Royal Crescent. But before you break down in tears at the prospect of a wasted and empty future, take some comfort in the knowledge that you can at least see how the other 1% live. Inside No. 1, they've recreated what one of these fine houses would have looked like in its heyday. Expect fine furniture, plush curtains and exquisite plasterwork. A sense of envy and unfulfilled longing comes free with every ticket.
🕑 *Tue–Sun, 10.30am–5pm*
🎟 *Adults, £5; concs, £3.50*

THEATRES

Rondo Theatre

St Saviours Road, Larkhall

(01225) 444 003

You'd think that a tiny, local theatre stuck out a couple of miles from the city centre would struggle to fill its seats. And yet, the Rondo seems to be habitually packed. People from Larkhall must really love going to the theatre. Or maybe it's that everyone in Bath has gradually realised that this place shows some cracking performances, and the tiny stage is so close to all the seats that it's impossible not to get completely drawn into the action taking place inches from your face.

🎟 *Adults, £6–£8; some concessions available*

Ustinov Studio

Monmouth Street

(01225) 448 844

Lordy, Bath's a posh place. While this does mean that the city can sometimes lack the cosmopolitan excitement of other, more diverse locations, it does mean we have some things other people can get jealous of; like Britain's largest puppet festival. Of course, the Ustinov has more strings to its bow than it would take to make an entire Muppets movie – challenging new pieces are the name of the game here. In fact, it's the perfect antidote to the sometimes stuffy and conservative Theatre Royal next door. Think abstract, modern performances and cutting-edge contemporary theatre.

🎟 *Box office, Mon–Sat, 10am–8pm; Sun, 12pm–8pm*

Theatre Royal

Sawclose

(01225) 488 844

A bit of everything to keep everyone in Bath's dramatic world happy. The Theatre Royal might be one of the UK's oldest stages, but that doesn't mean it's all Shakespeare and Pinter (though there are some excellent highbrow performances here). Instead there is a pleasant mix of high and low culture. Just imagine something by Stoppard cheerily sharing the bill with a camp pantomime and you're getting close to seeing how this place has remained popular with everyone, and why it is so often fully booked.

🎟 *Box office, Mon–Sat, 10am–8pm; Sun, 12pm–8pm*

🎟 *Prices vary*

Out & about

LIVE MUSIC

Moles Club
14 George Street
(01225) 404 405

Moles are a type of Mexican savoury sauce, often served with poultry, and frequently containing chocolate. Moles Club is a sort of musical equivalent, regularly serving up satisfying and meaty live acts, and now and again throwing in something sweet as a little surprise. Like Oasis for example, who, putting the finishing touches to a recording session, tried out their new material on audiences here. Roll with it? We don't need a roll, cheers – we're lapping this place up and licking the bowl clean afterwards.

Times and prices vary

The Pavilion
North Parade
(01225) 316 198

Honestly, there are some good acts that play here. We promise. Don't be put off by the dodgy Pink Floyd tributes and underage roller-discos. It's not all that shoddy. The trick is to keep your eyes on the local press, and there's a good chance you might stumble upon some properly famous band playing a bargain gig to loyal fans. If gigs aren't your thing, then this is also the venue for various themed clubnights, where you'll find nifty Nigel from your department trying to get off with veneered Vanessa from accounts while dressed in a school uniform. Now that's what we call entertainment.

Times and prices vary

Let's get physical

For a fun way to work up a sweat, head over to **The Pink Kitten Dance School**, (www.jnrhacksaw.streamlinetrial.co.uk, 07980 804 720) the South West's leading pole dancing academy. If the idea of acting like an aroused Abi Titmuss in front of strangers makes you feel shy, you can book private sessions for you and your friends, or even a one-on-one. It may be intended for girls only, but we're sure partners/ strange men you meet in bars will be very supportive of your new-found regime. Alternatively, if you fancy joining 50 Cent's street crew, sharpen up your moves with **hip-hop lessons at the YMCA** (01225 325 900, www.bathymca.co.uk). Beginners are welcome, but you may want to leave your bling at home to start with. Those diamond-encrusted dollar signs can be deadly in untrained hands.

Out & about

SPORT

Bath Cricket Club
North Parade
(01225) 425 935

Men in immaculately-pressed whites, a balmy summer evening, you, limp with too much Pimms, and then a roar as good old Chester DeWoolfe strokes the ball through extra-cover for the winning runs, just as the clock strikes five. Could there be anything more English? Luckily, Bath's cricket ground is a perfect spot for indulging your traditional sentiments. It's right by the river and, if you arm yourself with a picnic and a newspaper, there really is no better way to spend a summer Sunday. Howzat for a top suggestion?
Annual membership, £44; students, £22

The Recreation Ground
Spring Gardens
(01225) 469 230

How could you live in Bath and not get caught up in the insane, animal passion for rugger that infects the city every time there's a game on? Rugby is a way of life in the city. People live and breathe scrums and field goals and lineouts. Unsurprisingly, all the schools in the area ignore typical softie sports like football, and instead give their kids the chance to beat the hell out of each other every weekend. The Bath team itself might not be the powerhouse it once was, but watching a game at their home ground will still give you a real insight into Bath's collective psyche/psycho.
Tickets, £15–£30

Bath Leisure Centre
North Parade Road
(01225) 462 563

Why do leisure centres all smell exactly the same? We don't know, but it worries us. They also all look the same. All those strips of neon lights make everyone, however healthy, look like zombies. Still, if you can't imagine a weekend without your exercise kick, this is probably your best bet. There's a pool, squash courts, and a hall for basketball and badminton. All pretty standard really, though the gym is also used by the Bath rugby team, so there will probably be some really big sweaty men for you to aspire to be like as you pound the treadmill.
Mon–Sat, 7am–7pm; Sun, 8am–8pm
Gym, £5.90; swim, £3.20

FURTHER AFIELD

Bradford On Avon

Surely nowhere could be quainter and more ridiculously well-kept than Bath? Think again. Ten miles away, Bradford On Avon might just be the place that manages to beat Bath at its own game. A tiny, medieval wool town, this place has narrow streets with silly names like The Shambles, lovely little pubs, more antique and charity shops than you could ever believe necessary and the best tearooms in the country. Which all makes for a smashing day out if you're looking for somewhere that's more like home than, err, home. Plus the river is more picturesque and less polluted here, so take that Bath.

Warleigh Weir

Claverton

Just imagine: it's a blazingly hot summer's day and Bath is melting in the heat. Yet the town seems strangely empty. Where is everyone? Let us enlighten you. On days where Britain is blessed with tropical levels of sunshine, everyone has probably upped-sticks and headed ten minutes out of the city to what is simply called The Weir. All it is is a large shady field and the deep pool behind a picturesque dam. But, come el scorchio, it'll be packed with happy families and teenagers jumping out of the trees to impress some girls. It all makes for a lovely day out. Take the X4 bus and get off when you see all the cars parked along the roadside for no apparent reason.

Bristol

A bit like a big brother who's always at hand when you need to liven things up a bit, Bristol is just a 12 minute train ride away from sleepy old Bath. Brizzle offers everything you'd expect from a seething metropolis; you'll find plenty of clubs, bars, restaurants, shops, art galleries and young people with funny haircuts that are longer on one side than the other. If you're sick of Bath's rather serious approach to 'fun things for tourists to do' you'll find plenty of entertainment of the non-stuffy kind; there's a zoo, hands-on science museum and an IMAX cinema. If you want more information, we recommend you go out and buy Itchy's rather great guide to the city. Trust us, your grandchildren will love the story of that time you went to see the bright lights.

Out & about

TOURIST ATTRACTIONS

The American Museum

Claverton Manor
(01225) 460 503

We're not sure why there is a museum dedicated the good old US of A right in the heart of one of the most English cities you'll ever find. Whatever the reason, the grand manor house has a very fine set of gardens, some interesting artsy crafty American folksy stuff, and a nice little teashop where your gran can have a well-earned rest. Throughout the year, strange men dress in period gear and stage accurate, but slightly sad, re-enactments of that little tiff they call the Civil War. Swell stuff.

🕒 *Mar–Oct, Tue–Sun, 12pm–5pm*
💷 *Adults, £6.50; concessions, £6*

Bath Abbey

Abbey Churchyard
(01225) 422 462

Bath's abbey is pretty hard to miss really. It's one of the country's finest Norman churches, built nearly a thousand years ago, and home to some important moments in British history (the first king of a united England was crowned here, and Itchy's mate got off with Big Bertha on the steps back in sixth form). It dominates the skyline of the city from every angle, especially at night when it is lit up in a fetching manner. The tours and choral performances are good too, if that sort of thing floats your boat.

🕒 *Mon–Fri, 9am–6pm, winter;*
9am–4.30pm, summer
💷 *Free, but donations are encouraged*

Ghost Walks of Bath

98 Lower Oldfield Park
(01225) 350 512

If you've had it up to here (we guarantee you an appropriate gesture is being made to accompany this sentence, though of course you can't see it) with the typical tourist side to Bath, then this little jaunt could well be the perfect antidote to all those tiles and teas. You meet outside the Garrick's Head, and then an experienced guide will take you walking through the city's streets and terrify you with tales of spooky goings on in what you thought was a rather genteel town. Then it's back to the pub for a dram of something to calm the nerves.

🕒 *Tours leave at 8pm from*
outside The Garrick's Head
💷 *Adults, £6*

The Pump Rooms

Abbey Churchyard

(01225) 477 782

If the baths show off the ancient side to Bath's appeal as a tourist destination, then The Pump Rooms are a testament to the city's 18th century glory. It was in this fine salon that, for 200-odd years, the great and the good all got together to chat about how fetching Mr Darcy looked in his tight new britches, and how many pounds a year Colonel So-and-so was worth. Nowadays, it's a very fine, though very expensive tearoom. The biggest draw is still the famed Bath water, which is supposed to be very good for your insides, but in reality tastes like rotten eggs.

🄳 *Free*

The Roman Baths

Abbey Churchyard

(01225) 477 785

It's amazing if you think about it; a couple of hot springs are really the only reason this whole city exists. Nowadays though, these ancient pools are expensive, packed come the tourist invasion that takes place in summer, and to top it all off, you're not even allowed to go swimming since they discovered the lead lining isn't great for your heath. Still, you have to go, so there's no point bitching about it. We suggest you take the audio tour and discover again your childhood fascination with the Romans. Salve puella and all that.

🄲 *Nov–Feb, 9.30am–4.30pm; Mar–Jun & Sep–Oct, 9am–5pm; Jul–Aug, 9am–9pm*

🄳 *Adults, £9.50; students, £8.50*

Out & about

Thermae Bath Spa

The Hetling Pump Room,
Hot Bath Street
(01225) 331 234

Finally, about six years late and loads of money over budget, Bath's thermal spa place is now open and is absolutely amazing. It is, apparently, the UK's only natural spa, which makes it pretty special. If that wasn't enough, the building housing the ancient waters is thoroughly state-of-the-art, and the views from the rooftop pool are nothing short of spectacular. It's bloody pricey, but if you're ever in need of some sheer luxury, you'll not do better than a good long soak in here.

Mon–Sun, 9am–10pm
Spa taster session, £58 for two hours

Stag & hen

Illustration by Thomas Denbigh

TAKE YOUR PECK FROM ITCHY'S ALTERNATIVE HEN IDEAS OR THROW A SIMPLY STAGGERING STAG DO. WELL, STAGGERING IS SURE TO BE INVOLVED SOMEWHERE ALONG THE LINE...

Unless the bride/groom's into the type of swinging that doesn't happen in park play areas (if it does – hell, you need to move to a better estate), by saying 'I do' your friend is promising not to indulge in bratwurst boxing with anyone but their chosen partner. For £52 per person, you can make sure they pack in the porking prior to the big day at a sausage-making course (www.osneylodgefarm.co.uk), and fry up the results the morning after to calm your hangovers.

As they're already selflessly donating themselves to someone else for life, chuck some extra charity in the mix; if you can raise enough cash for a good cause, experiences like bungee jumping, fire walking and skydiving are absolutely free. Wedding guests could pledge sponsorship as part of their gifts to the couple, and the money saved could go towards an extra few days on the honeymoon. Suitable charities for those getting hitched to munters include the Royal National Institute of the Blind or Battersea Dogs' Home.

ALMOST MARRIED

L

Itchy

Calling all aspiring scribblers and snappers...

We need cheeky writers and hawk-eyed photographers to contribute their sparkling talents to the Itchy city guides and websites. We want the inside track on the bars, pubs, clubs and restaurants in your city, as well as longer features and dynamic pictures to represent the comedy, art, music, theatre, cinema and sport scenes.

If you're interested in getting involved, please send examples of your writing or photography to: editor@itchymedia.co.uk, clearly stating which city you can work in. All work will be fully credited.

Bath/Birmingham/Brighton/Bristol/Cambridge/Cardiff/Edinburgh/ Glasgow/Leeds/Liverpool/London/Manchester/ Nottingham/Oxford/Sheffield/York

Laters

Laters

Shopping

If the idea of late night shopping conjures up images of New Yorkers ambling around a snowy Fifth Avenue, then Bath's going to be something of a disappointment to you. Here it means an extra hour on a Thursday night, and even then, it's only going to be the biggest chain stores that keep their doors open. If you find yourself racing against the clock in search of an outfit or some last minute gifts then Jolly's (7–14 Milsom Street, 01225 462 811), Oasis (2 Cheap Street, 01225 442 922) and HMV (13–15 Stall Street, 01225 466 681) are probably your best bets.

Last-minute beauty treatments

You've managed to score a last-minute hot date. Well done, but look at the state of you. Fear not, Bath's therapists are on hand to transform you from beast to beauty. The Health and Beauty Centre (5 Old King Street, 01225 310 014) is open late, and on Sundays, for a full range of beauty treatments. If it's your barnet that's in need of some TLC, then Toni & Guy (2 New Bond Street Buildings, 01225 484 284) stays open 'til about 9 o'clock. The newly opened Thermae Bath Spa complex (Hot Bath Street, 01225 331 234) stays open until 10pm most days of the week for top-end polishings.

Food

There are plenty of options for post-club munching material. Obviously some are much better than others, so, in the spirit of journalistic enquiry, Itchy's intrepid reporters braved the cold night and sampled all the takeaways in town. Marmaris (4–5 Grand Parade 01225 461 946) is always jam-packed at weekends. Their chicken kebab is so good we've been known to have one for lunch without being drunk. Too lazy/wasted to even leave your own home? Don't worry as good ol' Dominos (66 Walcot Street, 01225 421 421) or Perfect Pizza (2 Grand Parade, 01225 447 037) will come to your door until midnight. There's a bit of a burger battle going on in Bath. Some will swear blind that Mr D's (8 St George's Place, 01225 425 204) is by far the best place to get one. They will happily give you a grease fix until 3am at the weekend so gain extra brownie points for endurance. Though they shut at midnight, Schwartz Bros (102 Walcot Street, 01225 463 613) take some beating in terms of taste, while locals in the know will tell you to make the effort and walk to Widcombe for Manhattan Burger Bar (23 Claverton Buildings, 01225 447 365). Your verdict is of great interest to us, so let us know who you think is Bath's burger king.

Laters

Late-night booze

You've had a great night, but now you're sobering up, and to extend the fun, you need more booze. Fast. The Huntsman (1 Terrace Walk, 01225 482 900) will give you alcohol 'til 2am, because that's the sort of nice guys they are. Moles (14 George Street, 01225 404 405) apparently serves until 4am, but none of us have ever been able to get anything after about 3am. Later than that, and the new licencing laws mean you should be able to buy booze any time at any 24-hour garage, like the one at Sainsbury's (Green Park Road, 01225 444 737). Cider for breakfast anyone?

Late-night smokes

Whether you've just run out of cancer sticks, or you're stocking up for the next leg of your messy night out, you'll be pleased to hear that relief again comes in the form of the your 24-hour garage at Sainsbury's. Turn up about 40 minutes after all the clubs have shut and you'll find a sort of impromptu smokers' shindig as everyone in the area will have gathered to buy supplies before heading home for a ciggie. It's also good for finding if there are any cool house parties that you haven't been invited to. If there aren't, then why not invite everyone back to yours to talk filters and rolling techniques?

Fun @ night

DON'T WASTE THE GIFT OF INSOMNIA BY COUNTING IMAGINARY ANIMALS – GO CREATE SOME SHEAR (ARF) MAYHEM IN THE EARLY AM AND ENTER THE ITCHY TWILIGHT ZONE. WE WOOL IF YOU WOOL

Go jousting – First up, feed up for some insane-sbury's prices. As witching hours approach, 24-hour supermarkets reduce any unsold fresh produce to mere coppers; pick up a feast for a few pauper's pennies and buy them clean out of 10p French sticks, which are spot on for sword fights. Up the ante by jousting using shopping trolleys or bicycles in place of horses, or start a game of ciabatta-and-ball by bowling a roll.

Play street games – Take some chalk to sketch a marathon hopscotch grid down the entire length of the thoroughfare, or an anaconda-sized snakes and ladders board writhing across your town square. Break the trippy silence and deserted stillness of the dead shopping areas with a tag, catch or British bulldog competition, and be as rowdy as you like – there's no-one around to wake.

Play Texaco bingo – Alternatively, drive the cashier at the all-night petrol station honey nut loopy by playing Texaco bingo: the person who manages to make them go back and forth from the window the most times to fetch increasingly obscure, specific and embarrassing items wins. Along with your prize-winning haul of mango chutney-flavoured condoms, Tena Lady towelettes and tin of eucalyptus travel sweets, be sure to pick up a first-edition paper to trump everyone over toast with your apparently psychic knowledge of the day ahead's events-to-be. Whatever you do, remember: you snooze, you lose.

Illustration by Thomas Denbigh

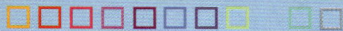

Sleep

Sleep

SWANKY

Queensberry Hotel
Russell Street
(01225) 447 928

With its central, yet quiet location, this is perfection in hotel form. Alright, so maybe that's an exaggeration, but it's berry nice.
🛏 *Rooms, from £170*

The Royal Crescent Hotel
16 Royal Crescent
(01225) 823 333

This is the proverbial 'it' when it comes to swanky Bath hotels; whenever there is some period drama being filmed on Bath's picturesque streets you can be sure some stars are kipping here.
🛏 *Rooms, from £199*

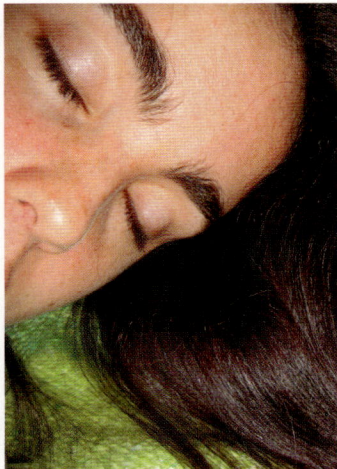

MID-RANGE

Apsley House Hotel
Newbridge Hill
(01225) 336 966

The beauty of this place is that you've got the tranquillity of a country house hotel, but it's only 20 minutes' walk from the city centre.
🛏 *Rooms, from £65*

The Ayrlington
24–25 Pulteney Road
(01225) 425 495

Close enough to the centre for all that touristy stuff, but far enough away that you can get a night's sleep without the drunks waking you as they decorate the neighbourhood cars with traffic cones.
🛏 *Rooms, from £75*

Dorian House
1 Upper Oldfield Park
(01225) 426 336

How many hotels are run by someone who is the Principal Cellist with the London Symphony Orchestra? If you want moving symphonies with your morning muesli, then this is the place for you.
🛏 *Rooms, from £65*

Pratt's Hotel
South Parade
(01225) 460 441

A splendidly located and comfortable establishment with a great name – when you tell people about your Bath break you'll be able to start all your tales with, 'We fitted right in at Pratt's...'.
🛏 *Rooms, from £55*

CHEAP

Bath Backpackers Hotel
13 Pierrepont Street
(01225) 466 787
You're sure to meet people who are as keen for a couple of 'cold ones' as you are.
🛏 *Mixed or female-only dormitory, from £12*

St Christopher's Inn
9 Green Street
(01225) 481 444
You know what you're in for when a hostel has a large, bustling bar below it. Not the ideal location for a quiet trip with Auntie Mabel, but great for a boozy weekend away.
🛏 *Mixed or female-only dormitories, from £10.50*

YHA
Bathwick Hill
(08707) 705 688
With laundry, a TV room, games and self-catering stuff, it's like being at home, except you have to share with strangers and your mum isn't around to make you cups of tea after you drink too much.
🛏 *Rooms, from £12.50*

YMCA
International House, Broad Street
(01225) 325 900
The YMCA's been here since 18-something. Back then it was probably cold dorms with sermonising, whereas nowadays you get cosy rooms, a great café and a gym.
🛏 *Dorm beds, Sun–Thu, £12; Fri–Sat, £14; single rooms, Sun–Thu, £23.50; Fri–Sat, £28*

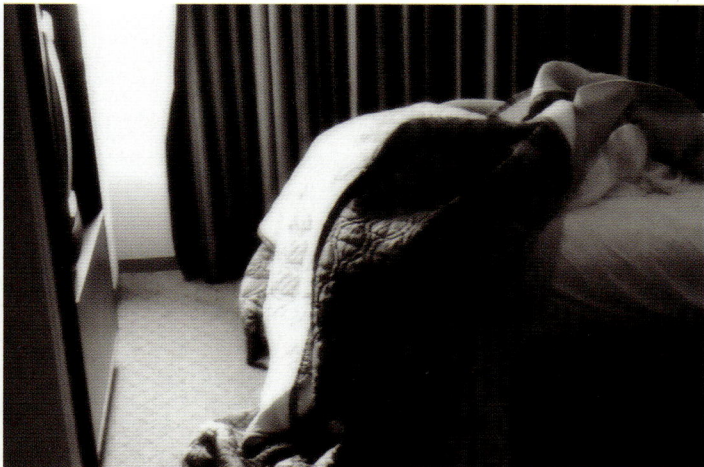

Itchy

Book cut-price, last minute accommodation with Itchy Hotels

Itchy Hotels has a late booking database of over 500,000 discount hotel rooms and up to 70% off thousands of room rates in 4-star and 5-star hotels, bed and breakfasts, guesthouses, apartments and luxury accommodation in the UK, Ireland, Europe and worldwide.

hotels.itchycity.co.uk
or book by phone: 0870 478 6 17

Useful info

Useful info

GYMS

Combe Grove Country Club
Brassknocker Hill
(01225) 834 644

YMCA Gym
International House, Broad Street Place
(01225) 325 900

TATTOO AND PIERCING

Kingpin Tattoo Studio
24 Vineyards, The Paragon
(01225) 463 707

Kingsway Custom Tattoo
2 Marsden Road
(01225) 758 111

MALE HAIRDRESSERS

The Edge
13a Westgate Buildings
(01225) 315 600

New Saville Row
14 Northgate Street
(01225) 310 110

FEMALE HAIRDRESSERS

Frontlinestyle
4–5 Monmouth Street
(01225) 478 478

UNISEX HAIRDRESSERS

Artizan
8a George Street & 5 Bartlett Street
(01225) 447 087/420 611

Toni & Guy
2 New Bond Street Buildings
(01225) 484 284

BEAUTY SALONS

The Beauty Connection
10 Green Street
(01225) 331 237

Imago
4 Abbey Green
(01225) 448 900

Tip-T-Toe
7 St James Parade
(01225) 462 265

BUSES

First Bus Company
(01225) 330 444

TAXIS

Abbey Taxis
(01225) 444 444

Bath Taxis
(01225) 447 777

TOURIST INFORMATION

Bath Tourism
(09067) 112 000
Almost as useful for the inside scoop on Bath as an Itchy guide. But not quite.

TRAINS

First Great Western Trains
(01225) 484 950

National Rail Enquiries
(08457) 484 950

PLANES

Bristol Airport
Leaving on a jet plane? After all we've been through? Well do come back soon.
(08701) 212 742

INTERNET CAFÉS

Click Internet Café
(01225) 481 008

Useful info

TAKEAWAY BURGERS

Manhattan Burger Bar
23 Claverton Buildings,
Widcombe Parade
(01225) 447 365
🕐 *Times vary*

TAKEAWAY CHICKEN

Dixy Fried Chicken
4a Cleveland Place East
London Road
(01225) 420 500
🕐 *Times vary*

FISH AND CHIPS

Avon Fish Bar
2 Lambridge Buildings,
Larkhall
(01225) 316 664
🕐 *Mon–Sun, 5pm–11.30pm*

Twerton Chippy
146 High Street,
Twerton
(01225) 425 920
🕐 *Lunch, Mon–Wed, 12.30pm–2pm; Thu–Sat, 11.30am–2pm; Dinner, Mon, 6pm–9pm; Tue–Fri, 5pm–9.30pm; Sat, 5pm–9pm*

TAKEAWAY KEBABS

Kebab House
16 Kingsmead Square
(01225) 461 915
🕐 *Sun–Thu, 11.30am–12.30am; Fri–Sat, 11.30am–1am*

MILKSHAKES

Shakeaway
3 Beau Street
(01225) 466 200
🕐 *Mon–Fri, 9am–6pm; Sat, 9am–6pm; Sun, 10.30am–5pm*

TAKEAWAY ORIENTAL

Sukothai
90a Walcot Street
(01225) 462 463
🕐 *Mon–Sat, 12pm–2pm & 6pm–11pm*

The Golden Dragon
2 Monmouth Place
(01225) 461 172
🕐 *Mon–Sun, 6pm–11pm*

Wan House
3 Victoria Buildings, Lower Bristol Road
(01225) 334 315
🕐 *Times vary*

SANDWICHES

Walcot Sandwich Bar
6 London Street
(01225) 310 099
🕐 *Opening times vary*

TAKEAWAY VEGETARIAN

Demuth's Vegetarian
2 North Parade Passage
(01225) 446 059
🕐 *Sun–Fri, 10am–10pm; Sat, 9am–10pm*

Support

Illustration by Joly Braime

ACAD (Advice and Counselling for Alcohol Dependence)
(01225) 464 374
16 Milsom Street

Bath Area Drugs Advisory Service
(01225) 469 479
1/2 Bridewell Lane

Citizens' Advice Bureau
(08448) 487 919
2 Edgar Building, George Street

Family Planning Clinic
(01225) 466 789
Sawclose Clinic, Sawclose
🕐 *Mon, 10am–1pm; Tue, 6pm–9pm; Thu, 9.15am–12pm; Fri, 3pm–5pm*

GUM (Genito-Urinary Medicine) Clinic
(01225) 824 617
Royal United Hospital, Combe Park
🕐 *Mon, 2pm–5pm; Tue, 2pm–3.40pm, 4.20pm–6.30pm; Wed, 8am–11.30am, 2pm–4pm (HIV clinic); Fri, 8.30am–1.30pm*

Hospital
01225 428 331
Royal United Hospital, Combe Park

NHS Walk-In Centre
(01225) 447 695
4 Cambridge House,
Henry Street
🕐 *Mon–Sun, 7am–10pm*

Police
(0845) 456 7000
Manvers Street
🕐 *Enquiries, Mon–Sun, 7am–12am*

Rape Helpline
(01225) 331 243

Samaritans
(08457) 909 090
10 Newbridge Hill

Somerset Gay Health
(01823) 327 076

Sainsburys

Charles St

Kingsmead North

Green Park Road

River Avon

Lower Bristol Road

Milk Street

James Street West

Monmouth Street

Sawclose

Avon Street

Corn Street

Bath College

Broad Quay

The Cross Bath

Westgate St

The New Royal Bath

Churchill Bridge

James' Parade

Lower Borough

Roman Bath & Pump Rooms

Cheap Street

Union

Union

Stall St

Southgate

Swallow St

Abbey Gate Street

York Street

Bath Abbey

Oran Grov

Dorchester St

Newark St

Bus Station

Abbey Green

Henry Street

Back Packers Hostel

G

Manvers Street

Pierrepont St

South Parade

North Parade

Parade Gardens

Bath Spa Station

Mormouth Place
P
Royal Victoria Park
Tennis Courts
Charlotte Street
Chapel Row
Queen
Square
Gay Street
Royal Avenue
Upper Church Street
Brock Street
The Circus
Circus Mews
Rivers Street
Assembly Rooms
Bennet St
ton St
Quiet St
Queen St
John St
St
Milsom Street
George Street
Bartlett St
Lansdown Road
Postal Museum
P
Broad Street
YMCA
Walcot Street
Building Of Bath Museum
Paragon
Walls
New Bond St
Green St
Northgate
P
P
Walcot Street
Bridge St
River Avon
Pulteney Bridge
Grove Street
St John's Road
Henrietta Street
Great Pulteney Street
Holbourne Museum

Index

Gazing at the stars

THERE'S NOTHING LIKE A GOOD CELEB SPOT TO MAKE YOUR DAY MORE EXCITING. HERE'S A RUNDOWN OF WHO YOU'RE LIKELY TO SEE IN BATH

From **King Arthur** (well, he was from the West Country, so we're sure he popped in to Bath when he wasn't busy slaying and questing) to **Moll Flanders** (look her up) and **Jane Austen**, famous people loved the city. And today it's not that different.

Recently, it was rumoured that **Johnny Depp** bought somewhere nice in the city. He joins shoe maker extraordinaire **Manolo Blahnik**, and *Buffy the Vampire Slayer* star… wait for it… **Anthony Head** (he played Giles) as some of the city's famed habitants.

Bath's also home to some of the brightest stars in the entertainment world. Electro gods **Tears for Fears** and **Goldfrapp** both hail from our fine city. As does funny man **Bill Bailey**. Unfortunately Bath has some dark secrets; keep it quiet, but **Ann Widdecombe** was also born here.

Finally, the fact that Bath looks like a film-set means it often is one. A couple of years ago *Vanity Fair* was filmed here, which meant we got the chance to see **Reese Witherspoon**, **Rhys Ifans** and **Bob Hoskins** wandering round in corsets and plus-fours. Too bad it's over, but keep your eyes peeled for trailers.